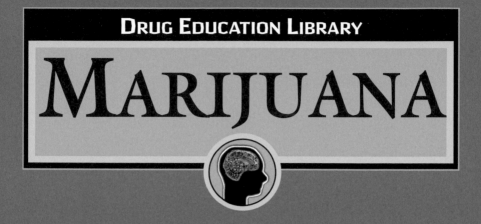

DRUG EDUCATION LIBRARY

MARIJUANA

by Hal Marcovitz

LUCENT BOOKS

An imprint of Thomson Gale, a part of The Thomson Corporation

THOMSON

GALE

Detroit • New York • San Francisco • San Diego • New Haven, Conn.
Waterville, Maine • London • Munich

LIBRARY OF CONGRESS CATALOGING-IN-PUBLICATION DATA

Marcovitz, Hal.
Marijuana / by Hal Marcovitz.
    p. cm. — (Drug education library)
Includes bibliographical references and index.
ISBN 1-59018-959-0 (hardcover : alk. paper)
1. Marijuana—Juvenile literature. 2. Marijuana abuse—Juvenile literature. I. Title. II. Series.

HV5822.M3M259 2007
362.29'5—dc22

2006017271

Printed in the United States of America

Contents

The development of drugs and drug use in America is a cultural paradox. On the one hand, strong, potentially dangerous drugs provide people with relief from numerous physical and psychological ailments. Sedatives like Valium counter the effects of anxiety; steroids treat severe burns, anemia, and some forms of cancer; morphine provides quick pain relief. On the other hand, many drugs (sedatives, steroids, and morphine among them) are consistently misused or abused. Millions of Americans struggle each year with drug addictions that overpower their ability to think and act rationally. Researchers often link drug abuse to criminal activity, traffic accidents, domestic violence, and suicide.

These harmful effects seem obvious today. Newspaper articles, medical papers, and scientific studies have highlighted the myriad problems drugs and drug use can cause. Yet, there was a time when many of the drugs now known to be harmful were actually believed to be beneficial. Cocaine, for example, was once hailed as a great cure, used to treat everything from nausea and weakness to colds and asthma. Developed in Europe during the 1880s, cocaine spread quickly to the United States where manufacturers made it the primary ingredient in such everyday substances as cough medicines, lozenges, and tonics. Likewise, heroin, an opium derivative, became a popular painkiller during the late nineteenth century. Doctors and patients flocked to American drugstores to buy heroin, described as the optimal cure for even the worst coughs and chest pains.

As more people began using these drugs, though, doctors, legislators, and the public at large began to realize that they were more damaging than beneficial. After years of using heroin as a painkiller, for example, patients began asking their doctors for larger and stronger doses. Cocaine users reported dangerous side effects, including hallucinations and wild mood shifts. As a result, the U.S. government initiated more stringent regulation of many powerful and addictive drugs, and in some cases outlawed them entirely.

A drug's legal status is not always indicative of how dangerous it is, however. Some drugs known to have harmful effects can be purchased legally in the United States and elsewhere. Nicotine, a key ingredient in cigarettes, is known to be highly addictive. In an effort to meet their bodies' demands for nicotine, smokers expose themselves to lung cancer, emphysema, and other life-threatening conditions. Despite these risks, nicotine is legal almost everywhere.

Other drugs that cannot be purchased or sold legally are the subject of much debate regarding their effects on physical and mental health. Marijuana, sometimes described as a gateway drug that leads users to other drugs, cannot legally be used, grown, or sold in this country. However, some research suggests that marijuana is neither addictive nor a gateway drug and that it might actually benefit cancer and AIDS patients by reducing pain and encouraging failing appetites. Despite these findings and occasional legislative attempts to change the drug's status, marijuana remains illegal.

The Drug Education Library examines the paradox of drugs and drug use in America by focusing on some of the most commonly used and abused drugs or categories of drugs available today. By discussing objectively the many types of drugs, their intended purposes, their effects (both planned and unplanned), and the controversies surrounding them, the books in this series provide readers with an understanding of the complex role drugs and drug use play in American society. Informative sidebars, annotated bibliographies, and organizations to contact lists highlight the text and provide young readers with many opportunities for further discussion and research.

Marijuana: The Drug That Never Goes Away

Marijuana has been a part of human history for more than four thousand years. It has been revered by the ancients, praised for its painkilling qualities, and consumed by artists and writers convinced that it enhances their creativity. The drug has also survived numerous campaigns to wipe it out. In the United States, the government has tried to burn the fields where it is grown and stop it at the borders, and yet marijuana continues to flourish in abundance and remains very much a part of American society. In fact, in 2003 the National Institute on Drug Abuse estimated that no fewer than 94 million Americans over the age of twelve have tried marijuana at least once in their lifetimes. That is 40 percent of the population of the United States.

Such staggering numbers would seem to give weight to the argument that the drug should be legalized. Proponents of legalization compare the antimarijuana laws to Prohibition, the failed attempt to outlaw alcohol in the 1920s and early 1930s. From the start, the law was unpopular and widely violated. By the time Prohibition was finally repealed in 1933, few people could say it had served much of a purpose. Proponents of legalization argue that when it comes to marijuana, 94 million people cannot be wrong.

Nevertheless, state and federal lawmakers as well as the courts have been steadfast in making sure marijuana remains an illegal substance. Even an attempt by some states to legalize the drug for limited medical purposes has run into opposition from the U.S. Supreme Court. The Court ruled in 2005 that while it could be suggested that marijuana serves a legitimate medical use, the likelihood that the drug would be abused is just too great to risk legalizing it for any purpose. And so, marijuana remains illegal everywhere in the United States.

Many opponents of legalization contend that is the proper course. They point to the numerous health consequences that have been attributed to marijuana—such as lung damage and loss of short-term memory—and argue vehemently against any effort to legalize the drug. Says John P. Walters, director of the White House Office of National Drug Control Policy:

> The truth is, there are laws against marijuana because marijuana is harmful. With every year that passes, medical research discovers greater dangers from smoking it, from links to serious mental illness to the risk of cancer. . . . In fact, given the new levels of potency and the sheer prevalence of marijuana . . . a case can be made that marijuana does the most social harm of any illegal drug.[1]

Not Just for the Young

Marijuana is known by many names on the street, among them pot, grass, weed, and reefer. There is no question that the drug is a big part of youth culture. Rock and hip-hop stars sing about their experiences under the influence of the drug. Grass is readily available at rock concerts and raves. Each year on April 20, thousands of students gather on college campuses as part of an underground holiday that has been set aside to celebrate pot.

Those activities would suggest that marijuana is strictly a young person's drug. Indeed, in many people's minds the typical marijuana smoker is the stoner teenager who gets high between classes or after school. But that is a myth. A poll conducted by the Gallup Organization in 1999 found that 20 percent of teenagers eighteen and under admitted to using marijuana. Meanwhile, Gallup polls showed that 46 percent of people between the ages of eighteen and twenty-nine and 45 percent of people between the ages of thirty and forty admitted to having smoked pot. As for people over fifty, 14 percent said they had used marijuana.

Two of those over-fifty marijuana users were Anthony Rocco, fifty-nine, and David Richardson, fifty-one, who were arrested in suburban Philadelphia in 2005 and charged with trafficking in some 3,000 pounds (1,359kg) of marijuana. They were both convicted and sentenced to five years in prison. When they appeared for sentencing, Judge Albert J. Cepparulo said he could not help but notice how both men seemed to have fit so neatly in their otherwise normal suburban lifestyles. "If we were to meet each other at a ballgame, I'd have no idea that you were involved in this activity and yet you were both leading lives that were lies,"[2] Cepparulo said.

Perhaps a reason so many people become longtime users is that the drug is known to be both physically and psychologically addictive. Medical science has found few effective ways to break a pot addiction. For heroin users, the drug methadone can be substituted to wean them away from their addictions. But there is no substitute drug that works for marijuana. The National Institute on Drug Abuse concedes that the only effective treatment for curing marijuana addiction is for chronic pot smokers to avoid the type of activities that trigger their desire to get high. In other words, if they are invited to a party and they know pot will be smoked at the party, they should avoid the temptation and stay home.

This eighty-two-year-old joins a protest to legalize medical marijuana. The illegal herb is used by people of all ages for both recreational and medical purposes.

Imported and Domestic

Another reason marijuana remains a presence in American society is that it is the lone illegal drug that is both imported and produced domestically. According to the U.S. Drug Enforcement Administration (DEA), roughly half of all marijuana is grown secretly in America, while the other half is imported from such countries as Mexico, Canada, Thailand, and Jamaica. That means law enforcement agencies must develop domestic as well as international strategies for combating the drug.

The United States has often waged successful wars on imported drugs. For example, the White House Office of National Drug Control Policy reports that cocaine consumption

Cannabis plants grow along the edge of a field and forest. Marijuana eradication is difficult because the plant is grown virtually everywhere in the world.

has declined by 70 percent since 1990. That is due primarily to enforcement efforts waged by American drug agents in concert with authorities in Colombia, where most of the world's supply of cocaine is produced. The program known as Plan Colombia has funneled more than $1 billion in American aid to Colombian efforts that have identified and eradicated the coca fields of the South American country, which has helped reduce the supply of the drug that ends up in crack houses in American cities. However, because marijuana is grown in so many countries, as well as in all fifty states, American authorities have found eradication of the marijuana fields to be an enormously complicated undertaking.

And so marijuana has turned out to be the one drug that never seems to go away. Judging by the millions of pot smokers from all ages and all walks of life, it would appear that many people would prefer it stay that way.

Chapter 1

MARIJUANA THROUGH THE AGES

Marijuana has a long and colorful history that dates back thousands of years. *Marijuana*—a Mexican term that means "good feeling"—actually refers to the flowers and leafy parts of the plant known as *Cannabis sativa*. The chemical that gives marijuana its narcotic effect is delta-9-tetrahydro-cannabinol, or THC. The chemical is found in the flowers and leaves of the plant and not in the stalk, which is the fibrous portion of cannabis.

For centuries, the fiber from cannabis has been employed for legitimate purposes: It can be spun into a particularly tough cloth known as hemp or Indian hemp, which is used to make rope, clothes, and canvas. An oil that can be rendered from cannabis has been used as an additive in paints. Seeds from the cannabis plant have been used in bird feed. They have no narcotic effect on birds.

The resin that can be extracted from the plant is rich in THC. When dried into a powder, the resin is known as hashish or hash. One dose of hashish, which is typically smoked in a pipe, is said to have five to eight times the potency of a marijuana cigarette, commonly known as a joint.

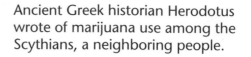

Ancient Greek historian Herodotus wrote of marijuana use among the Scythians, a neighboring people.

Cannabis plants have been cultivated for hemp as well as narcotic use for some four thousand years. Ancient Chinese emperors discovered the narcotic effects of the plant and urged their subjects to use it as a painkiller. The poet Homer wrote that Helen of Troy discovered the drug in Egypt and introduced it to her subjects. In the fifth century B.C., Greek historian Herodotus wrote about the Scythians, inhabitants of an island in the Araxes River who would throw their cannabis leaves into a fire, then "sit around in a circle; and by inhaling the fruit that has been thrown on, they become intoxicated by the odor, just as the Greeks do by wine; and the more fruit that is thrown on, the more intoxicated they become, until they rise up and dance and betake themselves to singing."[3]

Cannabis Arrives in America

In the 1200s, Marco Polo wrote about an Arab prince who fed marijuana to his guards to enhance their courage. Other explorers who visited Asia and the Middle East brought the plant back with them, introducing cannabis to the European countries. Cannabis became a valuable crop, both for its fiber content and narcotic effect. European writers were particularly enthusiastic about cannabis; in 1844, some of the top authors in Paris, including Victor Hugo, Honoré de Balzac, and Alexandre Dumas, established *Le Club de Haschischins,* where they could share their hashish while pursuing their creative interests.

Cannabis arrived in America with the Jamestown, Virginia, settlers in 1607. The settlers grew the plant because they needed hemp to make their own clothes—supply ships from Europe were infrequent visitors to the colony. In fact, the hemp crop was so valuable that colonial governments eventually ordered farmers to grow cannabis, extracting fines from them if they refused.

The evidence suggests that while the colonial hemp farmers did know the plant could also produce a narcotic effect, few of them were known to be pot smokers. George Washington, for example, grew hemp on his Virginia farm. Washington's diary entries report that he destroyed the leafy parts of the plant, causing historians to conclude that the founding father had no interest in consuming his crop.

When Marijuana Was Legal

Still, by the 1800s many Americans were using marijuana for its recreational purposes. It was occasionally smoked, but at the time most marijuana users achieved their highs by chewing and even eating the leaves. The more prosperous users could afford to visit secret hash parlors, where they smoked hashish in elaborate Arabian pipes known as hookahs that filtered the harsh smoke through water. In 1883, a Dr. H.H. Kane described his experience in a New York City hash den to the readers of *Harper's New Monthly Magazine*. The hash smokers, he wrote, "are about evenly divided between Americans and foreigners; indeed, the place is kept by a Greek, who has invested a great deal of money in it. All the visitors, both male and female, are of the better classes, and absolute secrecy is the rule. The house has been opened about two years, I believe, and the number of regular habitués is daily on the increase."[4]

At the time, marijuana and hashish were not illegal drugs in America. Although the rise of the cotton industry in the

1800s had made hemp a much less important fabric, cannabis was still widely grown on farm fields throughout the country. In fact, in 1914 Congress passed the Harrison Narcotic Act, outlawing the use of most drugs for recreational purposes. Marijuana was omitted from the law at the request of the hemp farmers.

This French cartoon caricatures a writer hoping for inspiration from hashish. Famed nineteenth-century French writers Balzac, Hugo, and Dumas all indulged.

Outlawing Marijuana

Nevertheless, there was widespread belief among many leaders of society and government that marijuana caused trouble. In 1915, California became the first state to outlaw recreational use of marijuana. Texas followed in 1919. By 1937, all but two of the forty-eight states had passed laws banning marijuana.

In most cases, the state legislatures were prompted to act after newspapers reported sensational crime stories in which the perpetrators admitted to being high on marijuana. Typical was this story, filed by Universal News Service:

> Shocking crimes of violence are increasing. Murders, slaughterings, cruel mutilations, maimings, done in cold blood, as if some hideous monster was amok in the land.
>
> Alarmed Federal and State authorities attribute much of this violence to the "killer drug."
>
> That's what experts call marihuana. It is another name for hashish. It's a derivative of Indian hemp, a roadside weed in almost every State of the Union. . . .
>
> Those addicted to marihuana, after an early feeling of exhilaration, soon lose all restraints, all inhibitions. They become bestial demoniacs, filled with the mad lust to kill.[5]

In 1927, a campaign by newspapers in New Orleans prompted the Louisiana legislature to outlaw marijuana. Within days of the law's adoption, a New Orleans newspaper reported a wholesale arrest of more than 150 persons, "Approximately one hundred underworld dives, soft-drink establishments, night clubs, grocery stores, and private homes were searched in the police raids. Addicts, hardened criminals, gangsters, women of the streets, sailors of all nationalities, bootleggers, boys and girls—many flashily dressed in silks and furs, others in working clothes—all were rounded up in the net."[6]

At the time, marijuana was made available to users as it is today. Some of it was grown locally in remote and barren places where police were unlikely to find it, or it was imported: smuggled into America aboard ships that docked in large ports, such as New York and New Orleans. Some marijuana was trucked across the border from Canada. Most of the imported marijuana was grown in Mexico and other Latin American countries as well as in China and other Asian countries.

Still, at this time using or selling marijuana was not a federal crime. Throughout this period, Congress was much more concerned with abuse of alcohol than with drugs. This was the era that saw the rise of the temperance movement. Activists such as Carrie Nation were making the headlines by leading protests against saloons. Finally, the dry movement had its way, and in 1920 the Eighteenth Amendment to the Constitution became law, making it illegal to sell and buy alcoholic beverages in America.

Prohibition, which lasted thirteen years, was largely a failure. Mobsters took over the beer and liquor business, smuggling it into the United States from other countries or manufacturing it in underground breweries and distilleries on American soil. The taverns may have been boarded up, but illegal clubs known as speakeasies opened for business. It is estimated that during the height of Prohibition, some two hundred thousand speakeasies were in operation.

Along with the speakeasies, illegal tearooms opened for business. The rooms served a potent tea brewed from marijuana leaves or simply sold marijuana cigarettes to their customers for prices as low as twenty-five cents per joint. Mostly, the tearooms were found in poor black neighborhoods in inner cities—it is believed that no fewer than five hundred tearooms operated in the mostly black New York City neighborhood of Harlem in the 1930s.

Police in 1937 set fire to seized marijuana made illegal by the Marijuana Tax Act passed that same year.

With Prohibition near repeal, Congress did turn its attention to illegal drugs, establishing the Federal Bureau of Narcotics in 1930. The bureau's first director, Harry J. Anslinger, called for a federal law banning marijuana. He got his way with the adoption of the Marijuana Tax Act of 1937, which assessed fees on hemp farmers and outlawed recreational use of the drug. In fact, the law helped put the hemp farmers out of business because the fees were prohibitively high. During World War II, hemp was grown in abundance because all raw materials were much in demand, but following the war the hemp farmers could not afford to stay in business and pay the high fees. By the 1950s, the American hemp industry was essentially dead.

The First Federal Pot Bust

As soon as the Marijuana Tax Act was signed into law, Federal Bureau of Narcotics director Harry J. Anslinger assigned his agents to round up pot smokers and peddlers. The law went into effect on October 1, 1937. Eight days later, the first two people arrested under the act found themselves standing in front of a federal judge.

The defendants were Samuel Caldwell, fifty-eight, and Moses Baca, twenty-six. Both men had the book thrown at them. Caldwell, a small-time Denver, Colorado, marijuana peddler, received a sentence of four years in Leavenworth Federal Prison in Kansas. Baca, one of his customers, received a jail term of eighteen months.

J. Foster Symes, the federal judge who sentenced both men, told them, "I consider marijuana the worst of all narcotics—far worse than the use of morphine or cocaine. Under its influences, men become beasts. . . . Marijuana destroys life itself. I have no sympathy for those who sell this weed. In [the] future, I will impose the heaviest penalties. The government is going to enforce this new law to the letter."

Harry J. Anslinger was the first director of the Federal Bureau of Narcotics, established in 1930.

Quoted in Larry Sloman, *Reefer Madness: A History of Marijuana.* New York: St. Martin's Griffin, 1998, p. 104.

Anslinger's agents made nearly four hundred arrests within the first four months the law was on the books. The Bureau of Narcotics would carry on its war against marijuana for a few more years, but in 1941 America's attention was diverted to a much different war. With American troops fighting fascism in Europe and the Pacific, enforcement of the laws against marijuana abuse was hardly a national priority. When World War II ended in 1945, the troops came home to marry their sweethearts, start new lives, and raise their families in comfortable suburban housing developments.

The Beats and the Flower Children

Not quite everyone sought that lifestyle, however. Some of the men who returned home from the war had other ideas. They gravitated to New York's Greenwich Village and other hip city neighborhoods, where they lived with their girl-friends in tiny flats and spent their evenings in dimly lit coffee houses. That lifestyle would lead to the rise of the so-called Beat generation in the 1950s. Their heroes were writers Jack Kerouac, Allen Ginsberg, and William S. Burroughs. The Beats wrote poetry, listened to jazz, and smoked marijuana. New York writer Dan Wakefield recalled meeting Ginsberg in 1961 while researching a magazine story about marijuana:

> When I went to interview him, which I did several times, Allen opened a big file cabinet and pulled out reports for me to read on the medical, legal, and historical aspects of cannabis sativa. He was eager to help anyone who would write objectively about this drug he believed should be legalized, offering facts and opinions and background information, all in a friendly, matter-of-fact manner. To my great relief, he did not use jargon or hip lingo ("Like, you know, I was up-tight that he might jive me, but he was cool"), nor was he ever stoned when I talked with him, a possibility I also feared.

Explaining the role of marijuana to the poets of his own circle, he told me that "almost everyone has experimented with it and tried writing something [while] on it. It's all part of their poetic—no, their metaphysical—education."[7]

Wakefield concluded that marijuana "was moving from the back rooms of jazz bars and coldwater pads of hipsters in Harlem and the East Village, seeping through the walls of college dormitories and into middle-class consciousness."[8] It certainly was. Within a few years, the 1960s would erupt into an era of dramatic social change, and marijuana was definitely at the center of the counterculture movement.

College students rebelled against the authority of their parents and teachers. Campuses became hotbeds of radical thought. Students protested against the Vietnam War, but they also demonstrated in favor of civil rights, women's rights, and free speech. Thousands of hippies and flower children flocked to San Francisco's Haight-Ashbury district and other urban neighborhoods where illegal drug use was rampant. Young people used drugs in defiance of authority. Wrote essayist Andrew Peyton Thomas, "For the flower children, of course, the marijuana leaf was the emblem of a generation mutinying against parental authority and self-restraint."[9]

Marijuana promised a mellow, feel-good high that could deliver an escape from the hassles of school or the cops or the weighty issues of the day. Marijuana smoke wafted freely at rock concerts and campus demonstrations. At the Woodstock Music and Arts Festival in upstate New York, the *New York Times* reported that no less than 99 percent of the crowd of four hundred thousand concertgoers smoked marijuana during the three-day event in August 1969. Reported the newspaper:

A billowy haze of sweet smoke rose through purple spotlights from the sloping hillside where throngs of young people—their average age about 20—sat or sprawled in the midnight darkness and listened to the rock music.

The smoke was not from the campfires.

"There was so much grass being smoked last night that you could get stoned just sitting there breathing," said a 19-year-old student from Denison University in Ohio. "It got so you didn't even want another drag of anything."[10]

"They smoked quite openly, not fearing to be 'busted,' at least not within the confines of the 600-acre farm where the

Holding a sign stating "Pot is fun," Beat poet Allen Ginsberg joins this protest in 1965 advocating the legalization of marijuana.

In 1969, the federal government conceived a plan to sti-fle the flow of marijuana across the Mexican border. The plan, known as Operation Intercept, required U.S. cus-toms agents to inspect every car, truck, and bus that stopped at each of the thirty border crossings located along the 2,500-mile (4,000 km) Mexican-U.S. border.

The program was launched on September 21, 1969. Each day, thousands of vehicles were stopped and searched. Initially, the program produced dramatic results. In America, a genuine pot shortage developed. One Rad-cliffe College student told the *Wall Street Journal* that she switched to LSD because it was so hard to find marijuana. Said the student: "I really didn't want to try acid before, but there's no grass around, so when somebody offered me some [LSD], I figured, 'What the hell.' I didn't freak out or anything, so I've been tripping [taking LSD] ever since."

Operation Intercept was halted after just twenty days. Officials were concerned that the lack of marijuana prompted drug users like the Radcliffe student to turn to harsher substances. Also, the searches caused tremen-dous traffic jams at the border crossings; motorists had to wait more than two hours for customs agents to search their vehicles. What is more, the economy on the American side suffered. Because of the long wait at the customs stations, Mexican laborers refused to cross the border to go to their jobs in America.

Quoted in Edward M. Brecher, *Licit and Illicit Drugs*. Mount Vernon, NY: Consumers Union, 1972, p. 435.

action is,"[11] the *Times* added. In fact, spokesmen for the New York state police told reporters that they made few narcotics arrests that weekend. One festivalgoer who slipped through their grasp was the bass player for the band Country Joe and the Fish, who flashed his marijuana cigarette at a camera filming a documentary. Another headliner was folk singer Arlo Guthrie, who performed "Coming into Los Angeles" on the Woodstock stage. The song told the story of smuggling two kilograms of marijuana through the U.S. Customs inspection station at Los Angeles Airport. The song turned out to be a big hit for Guthrie.

Head Shops

Marijuana would not stay in the counterculture for long. Starting in the 1960s, savvy entrepreneurs established so-called head shops that sold all manner of drug paraphernalia to their hippie clientele. Among the products found in the shops were colorful and flavored cigarette papers, needed by

The smoking of marijuana can include the use of a wide range of paraphernalia such as displayed here in a Dutch "head shop," the usual name for such stores.

do-it-yourselfers to roll their own joints; glass pipes, known as bongs; and roach clips, which could hold the final remnants of a joint so that the marijuana smoke could be inhaled without burning one's fingers. By the 1970s, the head shops had moved out of cluttered inner city neighborhoods and into suburban shopping centers. In describing her neighborhood head shop, Tela Ropa, Pittsburgh writer Kristy Graver said, "Local high school kids flocked to Tela Ropa like stoners to a bag of Doritos. Before you could say 'peace-love-dope,' they blew their lunch money on incense, lava lamps and candles shaped like marijuana leaves."[12]

The U.S. Narcotics Control Act

Authorities fretted over the shops, but there was little they could do. The state governments had outlawed marijuana, and the federal government had acted as well. In 1956, the U.S. Narcotics Control Act set a minimum sentence of two years in prison for marijuana possession, although in 1970 the U.S. Controlled Substances Act eliminated federal jail sentences for the possession of small amounts (mandatory minimum sentences were reinstated by a law enacted in 1986). Still, the paraphernalia of the drug trade had not been regulated by either the federal or state governments.

In the early 1970s, states started passing laws prohibiting the sale of drug paraphernalia. Head shop owners were arrested, but when their cases got to court the charges were dismissed and the laws overruled. Courts ruled that the laws were too vague and did not specifically identify a glass pipe or roach clip as an illegal item. Indeed, most states adopted laws that merely suggested if an item could be used for the consumption of marijuana, it was illegal. Under the laws in existence at the time, the shop owners could claim that the paraphernalia had a legitimate use—every pipe, paper, bong, and roach clip on the shelves could also be used to smoke tobacco, which was legal everywhere. Judges agreed, and threw out the cases against the head shop owners.

One of the drug paraphernalia manufacturers arrested in Operation Head Hunter was Tommy Chong, formerly part of the comedy team known as Cheech and Chong. Chong and his partner, Cheech Marin, were among the biggest stars of the 1970s, known mostly for playing a couple of bumbling potheads. Among their movies were *Up In Smoke* and *Nice Dreams.* After Cheech and Chong broke up, Chong continued to act occasionally, but he also went into the paraphernalia business. His company, Nice Dreams Enterprises, advertised in national magazines, employed a team of glass blowers, and sold more than seventy-five hundred pipes and bongs over its Internet site. During the raid on his home, police also found a pound (454g) of marijuana.

When he appeared for sentencing, Chong told Judge Arthur J. Schwab that after a lifetime of marijuana use, he had finally given up the drug. "I play a loser for laughs," he said. "My movie, *Up In Smoke*, was made thirty years ago. I couldn't make that movie today. I'm not that person anymore." The judge was unimpressed and sentenced Chong to nine months in prison.

Actor/comedian Tommy Chong is shown on his way to court on marijuana possession charges in 2003.

Quoted in Torsten Ove, "Chong Gets Jail Term for Selling Pot Pipes," *Pittsburgh Post-Gazette*, September 12, 2003, p. A-1.

In 1979, the DEA drafted a model law that identified bongs, roach clips, and similar items as employed specifically for consumption of drugs. States adopted the model laws. What is more, in 1999 Congress passed sweeping legislation making the manufacture and sale of drug paraphernalia federal offenses punishable by up to three years in prison.

And yet, many head shops as well as the manufacturers of paraphernalia managed to remain in business for years after the laws were adopted. As small businesses operating on the periphery of the drug trade, they were hardly regarded as priorities for police and prosecutors, who were more concerned with the growing traffic in crack cocaine and methamphetamine. Meanwhile, with the growth of the Internet, paraphernalia dealers and manufacturers could remain in business while hiding behind anonymous Web sites. But in 2003, the U.S. Justice Department announced a crackdown on head shops and paraphernalia manufacturers. Programs titled Operation Pipe Dreams and Operation Head Hunter led to the arrests of dozens of paraphernalia makers and dealers.

Dangerous to All Ages

As Operations Head Hunter and Pipe Dreams show, decades after marijuana was first outlawed, authorities must still work very hard to keep the drug out of American society. The fact is, though, that they have largely failed. Marijuana is the most widely consumed illegal drug in America. All marijuana smokers face an unfortunate truth: There are some very real and dangerous health risks involved in pursuing their habit. For example, medical research has shown that smoking marijuana is just as hazardous as smoking tobacco. Chronic use of marijuana may also cause brain damage. But judging by the number of people who continue to smoke grass, those are risks most marijuana users seem willing to take.

Chapter 2

How Marijuana Affects the Brain, Body, and Behavior

Marijuana smokers experience the euphoria of a dreamy high that begins within seconds of the drug entering their lungs. Typically, they are stoned for two hours or more, then the effect of the drug wears off. Of course, the more pot they smoke the longer they stay high. In 2004, *Rolling Stone* magazine profiled Molly and Moppy, two stoner students at the University of California at Santa Cruz. Moppy told *Rolling Stone* that he smokes between four and eight joints a day. In fact, Moppy said, whenever he begins a semester he always looks for places on campus where he can smoke a joint before the start of each class. Moppy's intention is to remain stoned all day. "I have faith that I could write a paper completely stoned,"[13] he said.

Moppy told the magazine he gets good grades, but his girlfriend, Molly, admitted that she has failed courses. Indeed, many chronic users of marijuana find it difficult to achieve good grades. The drug robs pot smokers of their short-term memory, making it difficult for them to concentrate in class, on the job, behind the wheel of a car, or in dozens of other situations.

In fact, some studies have shown that frequent marijuana use results in a decrease in a smoker's intelligence quotient, or IQ, which is a measure of intelligence. Writing in the *Journal of the American Academy of Child and Adolescent Psychiatry*, psychiatrists Joseph M. Rey, Andres Martin, and Peter Krabman cite a study showing that on average, people who smoke five or more joints a week suffer a 4-point drop in their IQs. They write, "There is considerable data showing that marijuana use is associated with poor school performance, lower grades, less satisfaction with school, worse attitudes toward school, and poorer school attendance."[14]

Affecting Human Behavior

When the smoke from a marijuana cigarette is inhaled, the fumes carry the chemical THC into the lungs. The THC comes to rest on the millions of alveoli that line the lungs. These are tiny sacs that absorb oxygen and pass it into the bloodstream. Of course, whatever is mixed in with the oxygen is passed into the bloodstream as well. After marijuana smoke is inhaled, it takes only seconds for the THC to reach the blood.

Marijuana can also be eaten. Usually, the leaves are shredded and baked into food such as brownies or cupcakes. When the marijuana is swallowed, the THC enters the blood through the lining of the stomach. It takes longer for THC to be absorbed through the stomach, but once it enters the blood the effect is the same.

The blood courses through the human body and eventually finds its way into the brain. That is where the THC comes into contact with neurotransmitters, the chemicals that deliver messages from brain cell to brain cell, affecting human behavior.

Brain cells are known as neurons; each person has millions. Each neuron emits electrical impulses containing messages that control the body's functions. To leave the neurons, impulses travel along large stems known as axons and smaller stems known as dendrites. When an impulse reaches the end of an axon, it will jump over a tiny space known as a synapse on its journey to the dendrite of the next neuron. When the electrical signal makes the jump, the brain cell releases a neurotransmitter chemical to carry the message. Accepting the message on the end of the dendrite is a group of molecules known as receptors. These receptors can only accept specific neurotransmitters. This is how the neurons of the brain work together to tell a foot to take a step, a hand to hold a pencil, or the lips to form words so that a person may speak. Not all

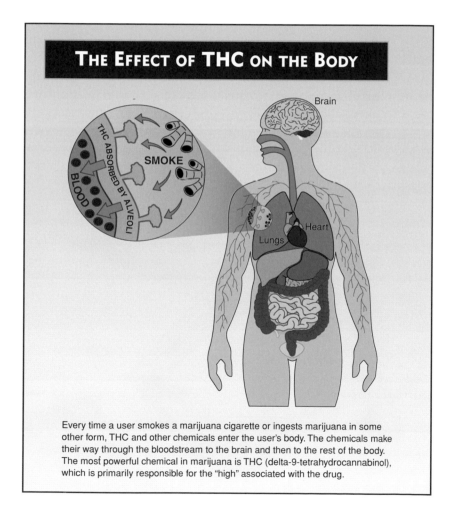

THE EFFECT OF THC ON THE BODY

Brain

THC ABSORBED BY ALVEOLI

SMOKE

BLOOD

Lungs

Heart

Every time a user smokes a marijuana cigarette or ingests marijuana in some other form, THC and other chemicals enter the user's body. The chemicals make their way through the bloodstream to the brain and then to the rest of the body. The most powerful chemical in marijuana is THC (delta-9-tetrahydrocannabinol), which is primarily responsible for the "high" associated with the drug.

neurotransmitters carry messages. Some neurotransmitters block unwanted messages from jumping from cell to cell.

A drug will influence the transmission of information from neuron to neuron. The drug may produce a flood of neuro-transmitters so that too many messages are delivered to the neurons. Or it may neutralize the neurotransmitters that work to block unwanted information, causing a flood of un-wanted messages to reach the neurons. Or the drug may act as its own neurotransmitter, sending its own messages to the brain cells.

When THC enters the brain, it bonds with the neurotrans-mitter anandamide. The combination of the two chemicals has been found to affect behavior in a number of ways. For example, as the combination of anandamide and THC jumps from neuron to neuron, it causes loss of short-term memory.

If this girl had been using marijuana, her ability to drive would be severely impaired by various reactions of the drug with chemicals in her brain that signal perceptual and motor responses.

THC also inhibits the brain's release of the neurotransmitter serotonin. Serotonin helps regulate mood, emotion, and appetite. When serotonin is blocked, the pot smoker experiences the dreamy, lightheaded, mellow high for which marijuana is known. It also explains why marijuana users get very hungry as they come down from their highs. It is the lack of serotonin in the body that causes what is commonly known as the munchies—the habit of pot smokers to consume large quantities of snack foods as the effects of the THC wear off.

THC is not the only chemical contained in marijuana smoke that causes changes in the body and the brain. In fact, marijuana smoke contains some four hundred different chemicals, many of which alter neurotransmitters. Some of them enhance the effect of the THC on the neurotransmitters while others affect the brain and body in their own ways. Some of those chemicals cause an increase in pulse rate, while others are known to cause anxiety and panic attacks.

Cannabis Dependence Syndrome

Many marijuana smokers are known to stick with the drug for years. In the brain, one of the neurotransmitters affected by THC is dopamine, which causes marijuana smokers to use the drug again. In other words, the stimulated flow of dopamine helps create addiction in users.

For years, scientists questioned whether marijuana was addictive, but recent studies have indicated that pot can truly cause its users to come back for more. Rey, Martin, and Krabman cited a study in which twelve marijuana smokers consumed the drug regularly for sixteen consecutive days, then were asked to abstain. They found that people who were asked to give up pot cold turkey exhibited symptoms similar to cigarette smokers who suddenly find themselves without their daily dose of nicotine. They write:

> Irritability, restlessness, anger, and sleep problems increased significantly on cessation of use. This is consistent with other studies, reports by young people in

residential care who were marijuana dependent, findings in community surveys, and laboratory studies. Thus, the symptoms and intensity of withdrawal in severe marijuana users appear clinically significant and are not dissimilar to those observed during nicotine withdrawal.[15]

Marijuana not only creates a physical addiction in its users but a psychological addiction as well. It means that pot smokers rely on the drug to lift their mood and help them get through the day. Psychologists call this condition cannabis dependence syndrome. As many as half the long-term smokers of marijuana are believed to suffer from the syndrome. What is more, chronic users find they need larger and larger doses to achieve the high they seek.

Driving Under the Influence

In addition to causing memory loss, the combination of THC and anandamide has another significant impact on the body: loss of coordination. That is why pot smokers often stumble around and bump into things. THC's effect on coordination can create a dangerous situation if somebody who is stoned on pot gets behind the wheel of a car.

In 2000, the U.S. National Highway Traffic Safety Administration examined issues surrounding drug abuse and driving at a conference in Seattle, Washington. The conference was composed of toxicologists, who are scientists that study the effects of chemicals and other substances on the human body and human performance. The toxicologists studied sixteen drugs and similar substances, including some that are legally available as over-the-counter medications as well as drugs available only through prescriptions. Also, several illegal drugs, including marijuana, were studied. The toxicologists conducted the study to determine whether people under the influence of those drugs could safely operate motor vehicles. The conclusion reached by the toxicologists was that

Chronic marijuana smokers who are asked to take a drug test are likely to fail. Among frequent users, traces of marijuana will show up in their urine for as long as fifteen weeks following their last use of the drug.

Drug tests are usually conducted through an analysis of urine in a process known as gas chromatography–mass spectrometry, or GC-MS. In gas chromatography, a sample of urine is treated with a gas that causes it to break down into its components and stick to a gel coated on the insides of the testing chamber. Next, the components are fed through a strong magnetic field that will enable the mass spectrometer to record their molecular weights. The results of the test are compared against a database of molecular weights assigned to different drugs, including THC.

THC is stored well by fat cells, which is why marijuana continues to show up in the urine of chronic users for several weeks. The GC-MS test can detect as little as fifteen nanograms of THC per milliliter of urine. A nanogram is one-billionth of a gram.

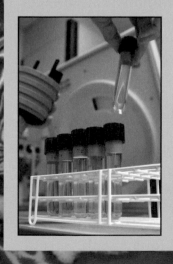

In recent years, members of high school and college sports teams have been expected to take drug tests. Many corporations now require job applicants to pass drug tests. Also, police officers, prison guards, and others who work in law enforcement are often expected to take regular drug tests.

Urine samples are prepared for testing for the presence of illegal drugs. THC can be detected weeks after ingestion.

users of marijuana should not drive, particularly when the drug is used in combination with alcohol. In their report for the Highway Traffic Safety Administration, the toxicologists wrote that marijuana

> has been shown to impair performance on driving simulator tasks and on open and closed driving courses for up to approximately three hours. Decreased car handling performance, increased reaction times, impaired time and distance estimation, inability to maintain headway, lateral travel, subjective sleepiness . . . and impaired sustained vigilance have all been reported. . . . The greater demands placed on the driver . . . the more critical the likely impairment. Marijuana may particularly impair monotonous and prolonged driving. Decision times to evaluate situations and determine appropriate responses increase. Mixing alcohol and marijuana may dramatically produce effects greater than either drug on its own.[16]

The toxicologists concluded that "low doses of THC moderately impair cognitive and psychomotor tasks associated with driving, while severe driving impairment is observed with high doses, chronic use and in combination with low doses of alcohol. The more difficult and unpredictable the task, the more likely marijuana will impair performance."[17]

And yet, people who consistently smoke marijuana can be found on the highways. Newspapers routinely report incidents in which drivers under the influence of the drug get into accidents, often killing innocent victims. Among the recent stories reported in the news include the case of Ralph Tarchine, eighteen, of White Plains, New York, who was charged in two accidents linked to marijuana and alcohol. In December 2005, Tarchine was charged with criminally negligent homicide when his car crashed, killing a seventeen-year-old passenger. Six weeks later, prosecutors said, while Tarchine was out on bail he smashed his car into a utility pole, crushing his legs. He was hospitalized for a month. According to prosecutors, Tarchine smoked marijuana before the first accident, then consumed alcohol before the second.

In Lake Worth, Florida, forty-five-year-old Michael Smith was allegedly under the influence of marijuana in 2006 when his car struck a woman and her two children, killing all three victims. Also in 2006, seventeen-year-old Curtis Clahassey pleaded guilty to driving under the influence and causing the death of another driver, fifty-nine-year-old Jerome Ratajczak. Police said Clahassey had been smoking marijuana, then lost control of his car, which crossed over the center line and struck Ratajczak's vehicle. Clahassey planned to start college in the fall of 2006, but he had to put those plans on hold while he served a year in jail. "This is a tragedy all around,"[18] said Kent County, Michigan, circuit judge Donald Johnston, who sentenced Clahassey.

And then there is the story of Karl Esposti, the fifty-year-old pilot who smoked marijuana before crashing his small airplane into a wheat field near Fresno, California. Esposti and two passengers were killed in the accident. A toxicology report on Esposti's body indicated that the THC level in his urine was twenty times higher than the level under which he could safely fly the plane, according to standards set by the Federal Aviation Administration. "How do you attain that number in the urine?" asked toxicologist Ernest D. Lykissa. "It's only through active smoking on a daily basis."[19]

Long-Term Effects

Marijuana users may start coming down from their highs after two hours or so, but the marijuana stays in their bodies much longer. In fact, THC can stay in the body for as long as ten days following the consumption of a single joint although it could take several weeks for the body of a habitual user to clear itself of the chemical. That is why drug tests reveal marijuana use several days after the drug is consumed.

But marijuana's impact on the human body does not stop after ten days. The effects of the drug can last much longer and even prove to be fatal. Marijuana smoke contains many of the same chemicals found in tar, the sticky substance in cigarette smoke that sticks to the inside of the lungs, eventually causing cancer. In addition to lung cancer, heavy smokers of marijuana also risk other ailments commonly found among tobacco smokers—bronchitis, emphysema, and bronchial asthma. In fact, the risk of developing those diseases may be higher among marijuana smokers, because marijuana smokers tend to inhale more deeply and hold the smoke in their lungs longer than the smokers of tobacco do.

The jazz trumpet player and singer Louis Armstrong smoked marijuana for years before his death in 1971. Eventually, the drug robbed him of his ability to blow into his horn. Said Armstrong's biographer, Laurence Bergreen:

This is one of the more difficult things about him to understand. He always said that he was old enough to re-

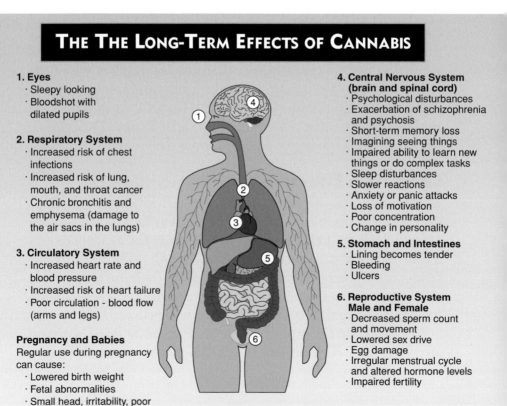

THE THE LONG-TERM EFFECTS OF CANNABIS

1. Eyes
· Sleepy looking
· Bloodshot with dilated pupils

2. Respiratory System
· Increased risk of chest infections
· Increased risk of lung, mouth, and throat cancer
· Chronic bronchitis and emphysema (damage to the air sacs in the lungs)

3. Circulatory System
· Increased heart rate and blood pressure
· Increased risk of heart failure
· Poor circulation - blood flow (arms and legs)

Pregnancy and Babies
Regular use during pregnancy can cause:
· Lowered birth weight
· Fetal abnormalities
· Small head, irritability, poor growth and development

4. Central Nervous System (brain and spinal cord)
· Psychological disturbances
· Exacerbation of schizophrenia and psychosis
· Short-term memory loss
· Imagining seeing things
· Impaired ability to learn new things or do complex tasks
· Sleep disturbances
· Slower reactions
· Anxiety or panic attacks
· Loss of motivation
· Poor concentration
· Change in personality

5. Stomach and Intestines
· Lining becomes tender
· Bleeding
· Ulcers

6. Reproductive System Male and Female
· Decreased sperm count and movement
· Lowered sex drive
· Egg damage
· Irregular menstrual cycle and altered hormone levels
· Impaired fertility

member when booze was illegal and pot was legal because of course he came of age in the Prohibition era in the 1920s. And the idea was—and he was not wholly mistaken at the time—that it was healthy. Well, it was healthier than toxic moonshine, which was making other jazz musicians sick and even killing them. And he felt that it relaxed him a lot. So even though he got into trouble with the law a few years later for possession of marijuana, he continued to use it in very heavy quantities, you know, three cigar-sized joints a day, at least, throughout his life.

Now, this did have a long-term harmful effect. I think if you talk to a doctor, they'll tell you that that mount of heavy, chronic marijuana use will have a bad effect on your lungs, for starters, and Louis did indeed suffer lung problems in his last, later years and couldn't blow for a long period as a result.[20]

Women who smoke tobacco are urged to give up cigarettes if they are pregnant, because the chemicals in tobacco smoke can affect a fetus. Pregnant women who smoke marijuana face similar risks. The chemicals in marijuana smoke can enhance the possibility of premature delivery. Studies show that women who smoke pot deliver babies with lower than normal birth weights. Also, marijuana smoke can affect the development of the brains of babies still in their mothers' wombs. Psychologist Peter A. Fried of Ottawa, Canada, has been conducting studies on the effects of marijuana on young children since 1978. He has found that the newborn babies of pot-smoking mothers tremble quite frequently and are easily startled. Also, he has concluded that by the time the children of pot-smoking mothers reach the age of four, they suffer from reduced verbal ability, decreased attentiveness, increased impulsiveness, and shorter memories. "On tests of verbal ability and memory, the children of regular marijuana users were significantly inferior to other children,"[21] he wrote.

Marijuana does not cause mental illness, but for years many people were under the impression that the drug could cause depression and even insanity, thanks to the 1936 film *Reefer Madness.* The movie tells the outlandish story of college students who become homicidal and suicidal after consuming pot.

The movie was originally titled *Tell Your Children.* Produced by a church group to serve as an educational film for parents, the film tried to warn adults of the dangers of pot. However, independent film producer Dwain Esper obtained the film, reedited it, and added new scenes. Esper made the story more dramatic and renamed the film *Reefer Madness.*

The film tells what happens to a group of students after they consume marijuana. One character, Bill, suffers from hallucinations. His girlfriend, Blanche, commits suicide. Another student, Ralph, goes insane, commits a murder, and is sentenced to an asylum.

Today, *Reefer Madness* is a cult classic. It is shown mostly on college campuses and theaters that specialize in screening art films.

A poster for the 1930s film Reefer Madness *falsely depicts the insanity caused by marijuana. The over-the-top film is now a cult favorite.*

Gateway Drug?

For years, sociologists, physicians, and psychologists have debated whether marijuana is a gateway drug, meaning it could eventually lead to the use of much harder drugs such as methamphetamine, cocaine, and heroin. One school of thought holds that marijuana is a gateway drug because the street dealers who supply the pot to their customers are usually in the business of selling other drugs. Therefore, the dealers encourage their pot customers to experiment with harder drugs as well.

But even without the street dealers pushing harder drugs on their customers, researchers believe there is a likelihood that pot can lead to other drug use. Rey, Martin, and Krabman cite a study in New Zealand that showed that by the age of twenty-one, 70 percent of a group of students had used marijuana, while 26 percent had used marijuana as well as a harder drug. They write:

> In all but three cases, use of cannabis preceded the use of other illicit drugs, and those using cannabis more than 50 times a year were 59 times more likely to use [other] illicit drugs. . . . It is possible also that using cannabis and enjoying it may encourage experimentation with other illicit drugs or that the use of cannabis may place individuals in contact with drug-using subcultures that facilitate access to other illicit drugs.[22]

Easy Access

One reason that marijuana causes so much of a health risk is because people smoke so much of it. Marijuana arrives every day by the ton, smuggled across the borders from Mexico, Jamaica, and other countries where it is grown in abundance. On the other hand, half of all pot smoked in the United States is grown in the United States. Indeed, anybody with a backyard or a basement equipped with bright lights can go into the marijuana business.

Chapter 3

THE CULTURE OF POT

According to the DEA, marijuana is grown illegally in every one of the fifty states. Marijuana can be found growing in backyard gardens or in basements, where bright artificial lights are used to mimic the sunlight that is vital to the growth of all plant life. It can also be found in sprawling fields hidden deep in backwoods country, growing in places where authorities are unlikely to find it.

In 2005, a police helicopter on routine patrol over a rural portion of Orange County, California, uncovered a marijuana farm located on a property roughly twice the size of a football field. When officers on foot investigated, they found more than two thousand marijuana plants, some as tall as 10 feet (3m). Jon Fleischman, a spokesperson for the Orange County Sheriff's Department, said the pilot spotted the field by accident, because the area where the marijuana was grown is covered by trees and normally out of view of aerial patrols. "It was only after narcotics investigators hiked up into the canyon . . . that they were able to determine this was a much more sizable growth than they thought," Fleischman said. "It was basically masked from the air. It was a very lucky angle that our helicopter was able to see it."[23]

For every cannabis plant that is confiscated by police, thousands more are missed. In fact, the National Organization for the Reform of Marijuana Laws (NORML) estimates that some 9 million marijuana plants are grown in America each year and that the marijuana crop earns its growers about $15 billion a year. That would make marijuana a bigger cash crop than wheat, cotton, and tobacco combined.

If people who grow marijuana in America are earning $15 billion a year, then there must be plenty of people willing to buy the drug. Statistics compiled by the U.S. Substance Abuse and Mental Health Services Administration (SAMHSA) report that in 2003, marijuana was used by 14.6 million Americans—6.2 percent of the population. There are

Law enforcement agents confiscate cannabis plants from a busted grower's field. For every plant officials find, however, thousands more go undetected.

more marijuana smokers than there are users of cocaine, hallucinogenic drugs, and Ecstasy combined. In fact, the agency reported, about 2.6 million people become new marijuana smokers each year. "This means that each day an average of 7,000 Americans tried marijuana for the first time," says a SAMHSA report. "About two-thirds [69 percent] of these new marijuana users were under age 18."[24]

Crossing the Borders

Although police often find marijuana growing in America, the drug is also imported into the country, smuggled across the border in a variety of ways. Marijuana is grown in Mexico and other Latin American countries, as well as Caribbean nations such as Jamaica. Thailand is also regarded as a major marijuana-producing country. These are places where the tropical climate and rich soil combine to make ideal conditions for the cultivation of the plant.

When it comes to growing marijuana, though, a tropical climate is not necessary. Marijuana is a hardy and vigorous herb, capable of growing wherever there is soil, sun, and rain. Indeed, marijuana is grown in abundance in Canada, a country with a short growing season due to its cold climate. According to NORML, Canada's marijuana crop is worth nearly $9 billion a year.

The most common method smugglers use to bring marijuana into America is to drive it across the Mexican and Canadian borders. Each day, tens of thousands of cars and trucks drive through the many U.S. customs stations along the two borders. Customs agents inspect many vehicles, but there are simply not enough inspectors to look through each car and truck that stops at the border.

Still, since the terrorist attacks of 2001 Congress has beefed up the ranks of the U.S. Customs Service, and now more cars and trucks than ever are being stopped and searched at border crossings. Since 2001, an additional forty-five hundred customs agents have been hired to help safeguard the bor-

Customs agents at the U.S.-Mexican border remove bundles of marijuana from a would-be smuggler's car. Border drug searches have increased since September 11, 2001.

ders against weapons and bombs that could be used by terrorists, but their efforts have also uncovered a tremendous amount of drugs. Indeed, the crackdown at the borders has produced results. In 2003, customs agents seized 1.2 million kilograms of marijuana, about 121,000 more kilograms than they confiscated in 2001.

With more customs agents looking through cars and trucks at the borders, smugglers have been forced to resort to other means to bring drugs into the country. Boats and planes are used, certainly, but the National Drug Intelligence Center reports that cars and trucks are still the major method of bringing marijuana into the United States. According to the agency, if the smugglers decide not to chance a crossing at a customs station, they can easily employ an off-road vehicle to drive across the thousands of miles of open wilderness that are available along the Canadian and Mexican borders. Says a report by the agency:

> The transportation of marijuana from foreign areas to the United States, as well as the transportation of foreign and domestic marijuana within the United States, occurs overwhelmingly by land. Transportation also occurs by sea and air; however, smugglers continue to exploit the breadth of the U.S. land borders with Mexico and Canada, transporting huge amounts of marijuana via official border checkpoints as well as countless unofficial crossing points.[25]

Sophisticated tunnel systems like this one, which has lights and a piped-in air system, are becoming more common for drug trafficking as surface smuggling gets more difficult.

In recent years, marijuana smugglers have turned to other means to sneak the drug across the borders. Since 2001, when the border crackdown started, drug agents have uncovered more than twenty tunnels dug beneath the Mexican and Canadian borders. In early 2006, authorities uncovered a tunnel a half mile (0.8km) long dug from Tijuana, Mexico, to the town of Otay Mesa, California, just across the border. At the entrance of the tunnel inside a warehouse on the Mexican side, police found several thousand pounds of marijuana awaiting shipment under the border. On the American side of the tunnel, which ended inside a vacant industrial building, drug agents found 200 pounds (90kg) of marijuana, evidently awaiting pickup by trucks. The smugglers responsible for digging the tunnel have not been caught. They used phony names to lease the buildings on both sides of the border.

The Tijuana–Otay Mesa tunnel was particularly elaborate. The smugglers burrowed some 60 feet (18m) below the surface. They equipped the tunnel with a concrete floor, a string of electric lights, and a ventilation system to keep air moving. They also rigged a sophisticated pulley system to help lower the marijuana into the tunnel. "The tunnel is absolutely amazing," said U.S. customs agent Michael Unzueta. "It is probably the biggest tunnel [discovered by authorities] on the southern border so far."[26]

Controlled by Gangs

The marijuana business is highly organized. It is headed by big-time suppliers who sell the drug to wholesale dealers, who in turn make it available to the street peddlers. In most every American high school, there always seems to be one student who knows where to find grass. What that student probably does not know, however, is that his or her connection is likely to have ties to a notorious gang whose members will resort to violence to control the local marijuana trade.

In some cases, the profits from marijuana sales are used to support political causes. In the South American country of

While waiting to cross the border into the United States, this driver reads a "wanted poster" for Tijuana drug gang members. Most drug trafficking is done by gangs.

Colombia, marijuana profits feed the coffers of such groups as the Revolutionary Armed Forces of Colombia, the National Liberation Army, and the United Self-Defense Force. Each group requires large sums of money to buy arms for their insurgent rebels, who seek to topple the Colombian government.

Elsewhere, though, marijuana exports are managed by drug lords who harbor no revolutionary causes and are instead interested in nothing more than money. Before he died in a shootout with Mexican police in 1987, the drug lord Pablo Acosta headed an organization responsible for smuggling tons of marijuana into the United States—often hidden beneath shipments of cantaloupes trucked across the border. Another drug lord, Rafael Caro Quintero, presided over a marijuana plantation in the Mexican state of Chihuahua known as the Buffalo. The plantation covered twelve square kilometers and employed some twelve thousand farmworkers who were responsible for cultivating, cutting, packaging, and shipping the marijuana north to America. The plantation was shut down in 1985 after the murder of DEA agent Enrique Camarena, who discovered the operation. Caro Quintero was sentenced to ninety-two years in prison on murder charges.

Even though authorities have caught up with major drug lords like Acosta and Caro Quintero, the marijuana trade never seems to slow down. Even after kingpins are caught or killed, others step in to take their place. In 2003, the DEA announced the arrest of Mexican drug trafficker Armando Valencia-Cornelio, who was charged with smuggling some 38,000 pounds (17,214kg) of marijuana as well as huge quantities of other drugs into the United States. A year later, the DEA arrested Rigoberto Gaxiola-Medina after seizing more than 1,200 pounds (543kg) of pot that Gaxiola-Medina's organization had smuggled into Arizona through a tunnel. Says DEA administrator Karen Tandy:

> Traffickers in Mexico move bulk shipments of marijuana through the southwest border by land, sea, and air. Drug trafficking organizations based in Colombia and Mexico move shipments of marijuana through the Caribbean to the eastern and southeastern United States on commercial and noncommercial vessels. Canada also has become a substantial source of marijuana, smuggled into the United States. Marijuana from Canada, commonly referred to as British Columbia Bud, is now available in every region of the United States. Since the demand for marijuana far exceeds that for any other illegal drug and the profit potential is so high, some cocaine and heroin drug trafficking organizations reportedly traffic marijuana to help finance their drug operations.[27]

Sales by the Ounce

The kingpins in the marijuana trade may be hidden behind fortified walls in Mexico, Colombia, or Belize, or they may

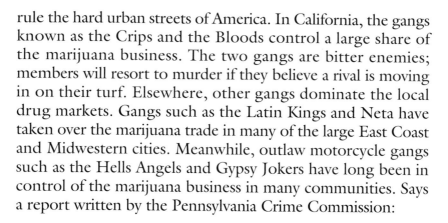

rule the hard urban streets of America. In California, the gangs known as the Crips and the Bloods control a large share of the marijuana business. The two gangs are bitter enemies; members will resort to murder if they believe a rival is moving in on their turf. Elsewhere, other gangs dominate the local drug markets. Gangs such as the Latin Kings and Neta have taken over the marijuana trade in many of the large East Coast and Midwestern cities. Meanwhile, outlaw motorcycle gangs such as the Hells Angels and Gypsy Jokers have long been in control of the marijuana business in many communities. Says a report written by the Pennsylvania Crime Commission:

> Law enforcement officials increasingly conclude that outlaw motorcycle gangs today are primarily narcotic networks, designed as continual crime-for-profit enterprises which gain their power through the use of fear and violence and through their network of biker contacts. Their major money-making centers around the manufacture and distribution of methamphetamine and phencyclidine and the distribution of cocaine, marijuana, and other illicit drugs.[28]

Whether it is supplied by a biker or a Blood, eventually the pot makes its way down to the street dealers, who sell it to friends or friends of friends. Typically, a dealer sells it by the ounce (28.3g), which is enough marijuana to produce from thirty to sixty hand-rolled cigarettes, depending on how much pot is rolled into each joint.

The price of marijuana varies from city to city. It is also likely to vary day to day. Like most commodities, the price is based on the quality of the product, its availability, and what the consumer is willing to pay. In many cases, though, the price also depends on how vigilant the local police are in rounding up street dealers. If the police are running sweeps, which means dealers have to be on the lookout for undercover drug agents making buys, then the price is going to be higher.

Sunlight is vital to the growth of plants, including marijuana. But when marijuana is planted in the sunlight, the growers risk detection by police, who have been trained to identify the plant. And so, many growers have been driven inside, where they have established "grow rooms" in their basements or closets.

To mimic sunlight, the growers equip the rooms with bright lights. Lately, police have employed infrared cameras to root out the grow rooms. Infrared cameras are able to detect heat. Sophisticated infrared cameras are so sensitive they can detect the warmth given off by the bright lights through the walls of a home.

In 1998, the PBS show *Frontline* produced a documentary titled "America's War on Marijuana," which showed how infrared cameras are employed to detect marijuana grow rooms. In Bloomington, Indiana, narcotics officers concentrated on a home where they suspected a grow room was in operation. Training the camera on the basement of the home, a narcotics officer told the show's interviewer, "That foundation's hotter than fire." Shortly after detecting the grow room, the officers conducted a raid and found marijuana plants cultivated inside.

Artifical lighting and fans create conditions for growing pot indoors in grow rooms like this one.

Quoted in *Frontline*, "America's War on Marijuana," PBS, April 28, 1998. www.pbs.org/wgbh/pages/frontline/shows/dope/etc/script.html.

Still, there have been some efforts by authorities to learn the average street value of marijuana. According to *Pulse Check*, a publication of the White House Office of National Drug Control Policy, marijuana smokers in New York can expect to pay up to $200 an ounce. In Boston, customers will pay $325 an ounce. In Portland, Oregon, the price is about $250 an ounce. Pittsburgh pot smokers can find marijuana for as little as $90 an ounce.

Celebrities and Pot

The people who are willing to pay those prices come from virtually every walk of life. Some are quite famous. In fact, the list of celebrity pot smokers is rather long. Occasionally, some have been arrested for possession of marijuana. Among them is the late actor Bob Denver, known mainly for his portrayal of the bumbling sailor Gilligan on the 1960s TV show *Gilligan's Island*. The late movie star Robert Mitchum found himself at the center of a Hollywood scandal when he was arrested and imprisoned for marijuana possession. The talented football star Ricky Williams has admitted to using marijuana for years; it has already led to a lengthy suspension from his team, the Miami Dolphins. Singers Whitney Houston, James Brown, and David Lee Roth, as well as rappers Snoop Dogg and Flavor Flav have been arrested on pot charges. The rapper Dr. Dre has long professed a devotion to marijuana. One of his biggest records, *The Chronic*, included several rap songs that praised the use of pot. Chronic is a street term for a particularly potent strain of marijuana.

Another recent album that has glorified marijuana is *Countryman* by country and western singer Willie Nelson. The cover of the album features green marijuana leaves—a design that prompted Wal-Mart to ban sales of the record in its stores. For his part, Nelson has never been secretive about his love for marijuana. In the late 1970s, he claimed to have smoked marijuana in the White House, where he was staying as a guest of President Jimmy Carter's family. And in 1995, he was arrested in Texas when police found pot in his car. A judge later ruled that the search violated Nelson's rights, and the charges were dropped.

Nelson intended *Countryman* to pay tribute to reggae, the style of music popularized in Jamaica by the late singer Bob Marley. Before his death from brain cancer in 1981, Marley was a dedicated smoker of ganja, the Jamaican term for pot.

Hollywood movie star Robert Mitchum is photographed while working on a prison work gang. The actor did sixty days for pot possession in 1949.

Country music legend Willie Nelson revealed that he had smoked pot in the White House while a guest of President Carter in the late seventies.

The cover of his best-selling album, *Catch a Fire*, featured a photograph of Marley smoking a spliff, which is a particularly fat marijuana cigarette. Peter Tosh, another reggae singer, released a hit single in 1976 titled "Legalize It," which called on the government to make marijuana a legal substance.

And then there is the story of Paul McCartney, the ex-Beatle who was arrested in 1980 at a Japanese airport when customs inspectors found a half pound (225g) of pot hidden in his suitcase. McCartney spent ten days in jail before he was released and kicked out of the country. At the time, McCartney was on a world tour with his band Wings, which he formed after leaving the Beatles. Angrily, McCartney declared he would never again play a concert in Japan. Years later, he recalled, "I was out in New York and I had all this really good grass. We were about to fly to Japan and I knew I wouldn't be able to get anything to smoke over there. This stuff was too good to flush down the toilet, so I thought I'd take it with me."[29]

McCartney said he has since given up marijuana, but while on a recent visit to Los Angeles he was approached by a group of teenagers who offered to share their pot with him. He said, "To me, it's a huge compliment that a bunch of kids think I might be up to smoke a bit of dope with them."[30]

Smokers Young and Old

When people like Paul McCartney, Willie Nelson, and Dr. Dre talk about their marijuana smoking habits, it makes national news. But as the statistics show, millions of other people in America smoke pot, and they do it every day—morning, noon, and night. Marijuana smokers can be found, for example, on many college campuses. In its profile of University of California at Santa Cruz students Molly and Moppy, *Rolling Stone* reported:

> There's always a little bit of surplus cash around for Molly and Moppy, because of Moppy's minor place on the great Northern California weed-distribution chain. He gets his

Several religions employ marijuana to help their members perform acts of worship. For example, during holidays some Hindus consume a drink known as bhang, which is a combination of milk and cannabis. They believe bhang helps them worship the Hindu god Shiva.

Hindus who found work as farm laborers in Jamaica during the 1800s introduced cannabis to the island. In the 1930s, the use of cannabis was embraced by a small Jamaican religious sect known as the Rastafarians, who believe marijuana opens their minds and helps them worship their god, Jah Rastafari. Today, it is believed that there are some seven hundred thousand Rastafarians worldwide, with most living in Jamaica and other Caribbean nations. About seventeen thousand Rastafarians live in the United States, according to a 2001 study performed by the City College of New York.

The Rastafarians' devotion to marijuana, which they call ganja, has repeatedly caused them trouble. In 1954, a Rastafarian commune in Jamaica was raided by police, who found more than 1 million marijuana plants under cultivation. In more recent years, Rastafarians living in Jamaica, America, and elsewhere have been prosecuted

herb from his friend Ben [not his real name] whose dad is part of a pot-growing collective in Humboldt County. Ben brings down about six pounds of pot a month, which he keeps in his closet in a safe the size of a gym locker. He pays his dad $3,000 per pound and generally makes $2,200 profit from selling it in quarter-pounds. Normally, when Moppy comes over to do a transaction, he and Ben sit with a bong, talking trash and truth, but last on drug offenses and often made to serve prison sentences. One Rastafarian told author Joseph Owens that even though the "government have it as a forbidden article, Rastaman deal with it because we know the good of it. Herb is part of our religiousness. It is that thing that enlighten people."

Rastafarians prepare spliffs of ganja, or marijuana cigarettes, for smoking in religious rituals.

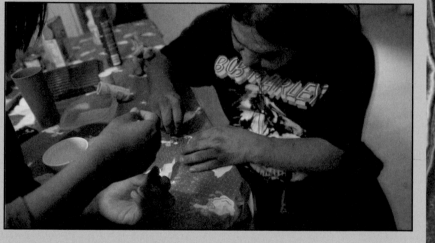

Quoted in Joseph Owens, *Dread: The Rastafarians of Jamaica.* Kingston, Jamaica: Sangster, 1976, p. 161.

week Ben had a cold and didn't smoke for a few days—for the first time in nine years, in fact—and now he's trying to stay off it. Withdrawal is bringing him down. "I wasn't expecting to sell in Santa Cruz," says Ben, as Moppy hits the bong anyway. "I came to school with just a little personal sack of weed. But everyone in my dorm kept coming over because I was from Humboldt: 'You're from Humboldt! I know you have weed!'"[31]

While it may be easy to assume that pot smoking is confined to stoner college and high school students, that is by no means the case. *Monitoring the Future*, the annual University of Michigan survey of drug use among middle school and high school students, reported in 2005 that 12 percent of American eighth-grade students reported that they smoke marijuana. Meanwhile, on the other side of the spectrum, author Larry Sloman wrote about encountering an elderly couple, Abe and Lilyan, while researching his book *Reefer Madness* (which has nothing to do with the film of the same name). Abe and Lilyan, who live in the middle-class neighborhood of Bayside in Queens, New York, admitted to being longtime devotees of pot.

Lilyan said she had smoked marijuana as a teenager, then gave it up. But when her own children reached their teenage years, Lilyan said she found their stash of marijuana in the home and tried smoking it again herself. She said: "I felt good. I felt that I wanted to talk to somebody, but there was nobody in the house to talk to. So I put on the record player and I started dancing and singing. I was having a great time. And that was it, my first time. I didn't realize till then that it was the same reefer that we smoked when we were kids."[32]

Lilyan said she buys marijuana from her nephew Mitchell, who often gets chewed out by Abe if he fails to provide his aunt and uncle with a high grade of grass. "Sometimes my husband curses at him, too," Lilyan said. "'You have some good pot and you have some bad. Now we want the good.'"[33]

No Clear-Cut Answers

Not all the marijuana that is either homegrown or smuggled into the country is used for recreational purposes. In fact, many people who smoke marijuana do not do it to get high from the drug but, rather, to help ease the painful symptoms they suffer because of debilitating diseases. Indeed, some effects of the drug have been endorsed by health-care professionals as acceptable treatments for plain and other ramifications of disease. For example, the dreamy, euphoric high that makes it hard for students like Molly to concentrate on their studies can also serve as an analgesic, meaning it is an effective painkiller. That can be an enormous benefit to cancer patients and others who suffer from long-term pain. Also, marijuana's propensity for making people hungry has surfaced as a treatment for the sufferers of acquired immune deficiency syndrome, or AIDS. In many cases, AIDS patients lose their appetites and suffer from malnutrition. By smoking marijuana, though, many AIDS patients regain the desire to eat.

For years, a significant debate has raged in American society over the rights of ill people to ease their suffering by consuming marijuana. The debate has reached the highest levels of government and the courts. But although it is illegal everywhere in America to smoke marijuana, many ill people defy the law, believing the drug provides the only true remedy to their pain and suffering.

Chapter 4

MEDICAL MARIJUANA

Marijuana had been employed for legitimate medical purposes well before doctors fully understood why ill people seemed to respond to its effects. Some four thousand years ago, physicians in China urged patients suffering from gout—a painful disease of the joints—to seek relief by consuming cannabis. During the nineteenth century, doctors believed marijuana could be an effective treatment for such ailments as rheumatism, tetanus, cholera, and depression. In fact, when Congress passed the Marijuana Tax Act of 1937, which outlawed recreational use of pot, pharmaceutical companies were permitted to continue manufacturing drugs that included extract of marijuana. In the year in which the Marijuana Tax Act became law, twenty-eight medications containing extract of marijuana were on the market.

Those medications eventually fell by the wayside as the U.S. government waged its war on drugs. Indeed, the 1970 Controlled Substances Act designated marijuana a Schedule I drug, meaning that the substance has no legitimate medical use. Even physicians who urged their patients to consume cannabis could not argue with the designation, because by then there had been virtually no scientific research conducted into the medical uses of marijuana. Until then, doctors had been urging their patients to use pot simply because they knew it eased their suffering, although they did not understand why.

By the early 1990s, as the AIDS epidemic swept through America and other countries, sufferers of the debilitating disease turned to marijuana, prompting influential medical organizations such as the American Medical Association (AMA) to issue a call for true scientific research regarding the benefits of medicinal marijuana. The scientific community responded; a number of studies were conducted, and most concluded that under limited circumstances, for a handful of diseases, pot could provide relief for patients.

An AIDS patient grows medical marijuana in his home.

Federal prosecutors have ordered the arrests of medical marijuana growers, but at one time the government believed marijuana did have promise as a drug that could treat pain and other symptoms of disease. In 1976, the U.S. Food and Drug Administration established the experimental Compassionate Investigational New Drug program. The program provides marijuana cigarettes to a handful of patients to gauge their reactions to the drug.

The first patient admitted under the program was a glaucoma sufferer. The disease causes a painful pressure on the eyes, and studies have shown that marijuana helps ease the pain. By 1992, the program was flooded with applicants who wished to participate. Rather than expand the program, the administration of President George H.W. Bush elected to close it to new applicants, although the dozen or so patients already in the program continued to receive their government-grown pot, which is cultivated in a closely guarded field at the University of Mississippi. By 2003, just seven patients were still part of the program. One of them is George McMahon, a Frankton, Texas, man who suffers from Nail Patella Syndrome, a rare deformity of the bones.

McMahon travels the country, speaking in favor of legalization of medical marijuana. He says, "According to the federal laws of this free nation, sick patients who use marijuana to ease their pain are labeled common criminals. In the meantime, people are dying. And I am dedicated to bring their plight to the attention of those who could change it."

George McMahon and Christopher Largen, *Prescription Pot: A Leading Advocate's Heroic Battle to Legalize Medical Marijuana.* Far Hills, NJ: New Horizon, 2003, p. 20.

Alice Ferguson is an AIDS patient from Connecticut who advocates use of cannabis for medical purposes. She recalled how she first learned that marijuana could ease suffering:

> My best friend in life lives in North Carolina. She has battled cancer in almost every major organ of her body except her liver. I mean, she's had it all. I can remember when we were 17, and we got back to her apartment, and she dropped to her knees with pain. I knew she had cancer, but I had never seen her collapse under the pain. I got her inside, and thought, "What could I do?" I could light a joint. I can tell you without question that she went from total collapse to sitting up and taking a few puffs, to being ready to go back out the door.[34]

The public debate over the benefits of medical marijuana set the stage for a legal challenge that would eventually be decided by the U.S. Supreme Court. On one side, the U.S. Justice Department fought to uphold the Controlled Substances Act, which for more than three decades held that marijuana had no useful medical purpose. On the other side stood the sufferers of AIDS, cancer, and other painful diseases, who felt that they should have access to the only drug that provides them with relief and that they should not have to break the law to use it.

Proposition P

Angel Raich lives in a comfortable neighborhood of Oakland, California, where she and her husband, Robert, raise their two teenagers. Raich would hardly fit anyone's idea of a stoner, and yet she has used marijuana daily for years. She suffers from an inoperable brain tumor as well as a painful spine disease that confined her to a wheelchair for two years. In 1997, on the advice of a physician, she started smoking cannabis. Almost immediately, the pain eased in her spine, while she found that the effects of the tumor were also much

AIDS patients at a San Francisco co-op play bingo while they smoke marijuana to increase their appetites. San Francisco legalized such medical use in the 1990s.

less debilitating. Raich found that the marijuana helped her manage her symptoms, enabling her to lead a normal life.

Of course, every time Raich lights up a marijuana cigarette she violates current drug laws. Still, Raich feels that marijuana is the only effective treatment for her pain. "If I stop using it I would die," said Raich. "I do not have a choice but to continue using cannabis."[35]

Raich obtains her marijuana from the mostly anonymous pot growers in northern California who provide the drug exclusively to cancer and AIDS patients and others who consume it to ease their symptoms. There are many such growers in that region. They entered the medical marijuana business in the early 1990s in response to the AIDS epidemic. San Francisco, with its large population of gays, has been hit hard during the epidemic. In 1991, a group of San Francisco gay activists established the Cannabis Buyers Club specifically to provide pot to AIDS patients. That year, gay activists also organized the drive to slate Proposition P on the ballot in San Francisco. The ballot question asked voters whether California should legalize medical marijuana. The measure passed with 80 percent of the vote.

Sometimes, medical marijuana growers have no qualms about identifying themselves. One of the leaders of the Proposition P movement was Dennis Peron, a gay San Francisco man whose companion, Jonathan West, died from AIDS. Peron watched how the disease robbed West of his strength and appetite, and also how cannabis eased his suffering. Following West's death, Peron established a farm near the town of Williams, deep in the northern California countryside. Peron grows pot on the farm, exclusively for medical purposes. "All use is medical," he says. "If you're smoking recreationally, just to get high, first I think you're stupid, and second, I don't have any time for you."[36]

Since Proposition P was limited to the city of San Francisco, it had no effect on California's state laws banning marijuana use. Still, the activists were encouraged by the response from San Francisco voters, and they urged the city's board of supervisors to adopt a resolution decriminalizing medical marijuana. The supervisors agreed, passing a resolution that stated, "San Francisco Police and the District Attorney will place as its lowest priority, enforcement of marijuana laws that interfere with the medical application of this valued herb."[37]

Treating AIDS and Cancer

Medical marijuana activists were not satisfied with their victory in San Francisco. Following adoption of Proposition P, Peron and other activists organized a statewide movement to convince the California Assembly that medical marijuana should be legalized. In 1996, they succeeded in slating a statewide ballot question asking voters to approve the California Compassionate Use Act, legalizing the use of marijuana by anyone who obtains the recommendation of a physician for treatment of "cancer, anorexia, AIDS, chronic fatigue, spasticity, glaucoma, arthritis, migraine headaches, or any other illness for which marijuana provides relief."[38]

Voters approved the measure, making California the first state to legalize medical marijuana. Within a few years, nine more states—Alaska, Arizona, Colorado, Hawaii, Maine, Montana, Nevada, Oregon, and Washington—would enact similar laws. A tenth state, Maryland, reduced the penalty for possession of medical marijuana to a small fine.

Legislatures in those states reacted to the will of their voters but also to the mounting scientific evidence that suggests marijuana does possess medical qualities. In 2001, the AMA issued a report summarizing the findings of a number of scientific studies. The AMA found, for example, that marijuana's propensity for making its users hungry could be an enormous benefit to AIDS sufferers, who are often made

A medical marijuana activist displays a bowl with joints for medical use and a slogan referring to the push to legalize such use, which is still highly controversial.

We are out to change the world and change the world, we will! We'll do it with amazing grace, compassion, faith and skill!

nauseated by the disease as well as the harsh drugs used to treat the ailment. Likewise, the AMA found, cancer patients forced to endure chemotherapy could also benefit by consuming marijuana. Chemotherapy is the aggressive use of chemicals to kill cancer cells; it can be an effective treatment, but when patients' bodies are bombarded by the chemicals, they often grow ill and nauseated and have difficulty keeping their food down.

Multiple sclerosis patients were also found to benefit from consuming cannabis. These patients suffer from spasticity, meaning their muscles grow rigid. Cannabis relaxes their muscles and gives them freedom of movement, the AMA found.

The AMA also found that glaucoma patients could find relief from cannabis. Glaucoma is an eye condition made painful by increased pressure on the eyeballs. Eventually, it can lead to blindness. Marijuana was found to ease the pressure suffered by glaucoma patients. However, in this case the AMA cautioned that marijuana may not be the right medicine for many glaucoma sufferers. Since many glaucoma patients are elderly, the association said, caution should be urged in the use of marijuana because the drug can also cause the pulse to race, a potentially fatal side effect for elderly users. Still, for younger and otherwise fit glaucoma patients, the association suggested that cannabis could be an effective treatment.

Finally, the AMA concluded that the single most important use of medical marijuana is to treat pain. For years, medical researchers have struggled to develop effective analgesics, and many highly effective drugs can be prescribed today for severe pain. But in most cases, those treatments are drawn from the class of drugs known as opioids, which can be highly addictive. In fact, the illegal and addictive drug heroin is an opioid. While marijuana does have addictive qualities, the AMA suggested that marijuana may be far less addictive than most opioids. The association recommended further study into the use of marijuana as a pain reliever.

A scientist holds up a bud of marijuana and a bottle of Marinol, a drug made from synthetic THC. Marinol supposedly offers medical users the same benefits as smoking marijuana.

Marinol

Medical marijuana advocates embraced the AMA report, declaring that an influential and respected national organization had now recognized the validity of medical marijuana. Still, the concept of legalizing pot for medical purposes had its critics. Sheryl Massaro, a spokesperson for the National Institute on Drug Abuse, said that legalizing marijuana for medical reasons could suggest to people that using pot for recreational purposes is acceptable and harmless. "Seeming to legalize marijuana for anything would give young people the wrong impression," she said. "That doesn't even seem to enter the minds of a lot of people who are promoting it for medical use."[39] And Medical College of Virginia pharmacology professor Billy R. Martin insisted that there are many legitimate drugs that can provide the same benefits as cannabis. In addition to the well-known painkillers, Martin said, pharmaceutical companies had recently developed drugs to counter the nausea brought on by AIDS and chemotherapy. "There are better drugs out there,"[40] he said.

One such drug may be Marinol, which has been used to treat chemotherapy-induced nausea since 1985. Marinol is composed of a synthetic form of THC. It is dispensed in pill form. Essentially, Marinol provides the stomach-soothing benefits of THC without getting the user stoned. Also, since it is not smoked, Marinol cannot damage the lungs of the user.

Critics believe Marinol has its shortcomings and is far less effective than marijuana. For example, since it enters the blood through the stomach lining, Marinol takes far more time to work. Asking an AIDS or cancer patient to spend a few more minutes waiting for relief may not seem like much to ask, but the patient who is enduring wrenching nausea or chronic vomiting may disagree.

What is more, Marinol may not get the patient stoned, but it does put the user to

A microscopic view reveals THC crystals on a cannabis bud.

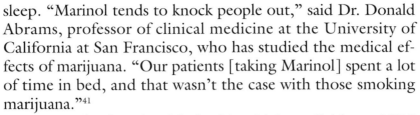

sleep. "Marinol tends to knock people out," said Dr. Donald Abrams, professor of clinical medicine at the University of California at San Francisco, who has studied the medical effects of marijuana. "Our patients [taking Marinol] spent a lot of time in bed, and that wasn't the case with those smoking marijuana."[41]

Despite the fact that Marinol is widely available to AIDS and cancer patients as well as others, many patients have turned instead to marijuana. Many of them made the decision to break the law with the blessing of their doctors, who believed Marinol would fall short of managing their symptoms. University of Arizona pharmacology professor Paul Consroe said one important difference between Marinol and pot is that the medical marijuana smoker needs to smoke only enough of the drug to find relief, whereas the Marinol user gets the full jolt of whatever is in the pill. He said, "With smoked marijuana, patients get immediate relief, whereas with the oral drug they get a delayed, big rush of unpleasantness. When they take a small dose [of Marinol] it doesn't work."[42]

In the Wrong Hands

In 2002, U.S. attorney general John Ashcroft declared that he would crack down on medical marijuana growers. Ashcroft insisted that the 1970 federal Controlled Substances Act took precedence over the state laws that permitted marijuana for medical purposes, meaning that whatever the laws of California, Oregon, and the other states permitted, growing, selling, and using marijuana for medical purposes is illegal under federal law. He directed the DEA to investigate and arrest medical marijuana growers.

The DEA responded that year by raiding the Oroville, California, home of Diane Monson, who grew marijuana in her backyard garden. Monson started smoking pot to ease her own chronic back pain. In the raid on Monson's garden, the DEA seized six plants. Monson fought back, asking the

Angel Raich (left) and Diane Monson leave court after suing the federal government for stopping medical marijuana use in states.

In 2002, Ed Rosenthal of Oakland, California, was arrested, tried, and convicted of selling marijuana. However, the verdict sparked outrage in the community, as well as among some of the jurors who voted to convict the fifty-eight-year-old defendant.

Rosenthal sold marijuana for medicinal purposes only. All his clients were cancer patients or sufferers of other diseases such as AIDS. During the trial, U.S. district court judge Charles Breyer consistently ruled that the jurors should not hear evidence that Rosenthal sold marijuana for medicinal purposes. Under law, jurors are not permitted to read about the case as it is covered in the newspapers or other media until after the trial has concluded. After they returned a verdict of guilty, the jurors read the back papers and learned that the information about Rosenthal's clients had been withheld from them.

Five of the twelve jurors who voted to convict Rosenthal called a press conference to announce that if they had known Rosenthal sold marijuana for medicinal purposes, they would have found him not guilty. Since verdicts in criminal cases require unanimous decisions by jurors, their votes would have meant Rosenthal's acquittal. At sentencing, Rosenthal could have received up to five years in prison, but due to the public outrage over the case, Breyer sentenced the defendant to a single day in jail, which he had already served following his arrest.

Protesters demand the release of medical marijuana dealer Ed Rosenthal.

courts to prohibit the Justice Department from prosecuting the growers and users of medical marijuana. Monson enlisted Angel Raich as an ally. The two women filed a lawsuit against the Justice Department, arguing that the federal government could not enforce the Controlled Substances Act in states that had adopted medical marijuana laws.

A federal judge rejected the women's claim and refused to bar the Justice Department from enforcing the Controlled Substances Act on medical marijuana growers, but in 2003 an appeals court sided with Monson and Raich. The appeals court said that Congress, which enacted the Controlled Substances Act, exceeded its authority by prohibiting use of a medically advantageous drug. At that point, the Justice Department appealed the case to the U.S. Supreme Court. Arguments were held before the Court in November 2004; seven months later the Court issued its opinion. The Court ruled that the federal government does have the power under the 1970 law to prosecute growers and users of medical marijuana, despite what state laws may allow.

Supreme Court Decision

In writing the Supreme Court's opinion, Justice John Paul Stevens said it is clear that AIDS and cancer victims and other sufferers of debilitating diseases have valid reasons for wanting to use medical marijuana. Stevens said he was moved by the afflictions that plagued Raich and Monson. Nevertheless, Stevens said, it is evident that the amount of marijuana grown in the United States and imported from other countries is far in excess of what medical marijuana users require. Clearly, Stevens said, if the Court permitted the production of medical marijuana, it would not take long for the pot to wind up in the wrong hands. "The likelihood that all such production . . . will precisely match the patients' needs . . . seems remote, whereas the danger that excesses will satisfy some of the admittedly enormous demand for recreational use seems obvious,"[43] he said.

Advocates for medical marijuana were shocked and saddened by the Supreme Court decision. Angel Raich vowed to keep using cannabis. "It is absolutely cruel that the federal government does not allow us the right to use this medicine," said Raich. "It is not easy for patients that really need this medicine . . . to have to fight for our lives on this kind of level."[44]

Decriminalizing Pot

Raich and other medical marijuana advocates vowed to take their fight to Congress to amend the Controlled Substances Act, permitting the use of marijuana for medical purposes. Within a year, the measure had stalled. By then, Congress was embroiled in other issues, such as the war in Iraq, safeguarding the country against terrorism, and getting the national economy on track. The plight of AIDS sufferers and cancer patients seemed to be a low national priority.

Indeed, there appears to be little interest in the Capitol for legalizing marijuana on a national level. But that does not mean that marijuana users still face the long jail sentences that consumers of the drug faced a half century or more ago. Although marijuana still remains an illegal substance in all fifty states, there has been a movement among some state legislatures to at least decriminalize the drug. It is now possible in some parts of the country to be caught with a small amount of marijuana for personal use and to be released with no jail sentence, fine, or blot on one's record. While it is clear that some states have taken a fresh and liberal outlook toward pot smokers, the casual American marijuana user may be shocked to find that in other places on the planet, some countries have gone even further in concluding that individuals should have the right to consume cannabis.

Chapter 5

THE DEBATE OVER LEGALIZATION

In some states, possession of even a small amount of marijuana is a crime punishable by a jail sentence. But that is only the start of troubles for the marijuana offender, particularly if he or she is young. An arrest record can follow a person for the rest of his or her life. Employers will turn down applicants who have criminal records, even if the offense involved possession of no more than a single marijuana cigarette. What is more, since 1998 the federal government has denied student loans to applicants who have been convicted in drug cases. Denial of financial aid could hinder a student's chances of obtaining a college education.

There has been a growing attitude in America that such treatment for the marijuana offender is both harsh and unfair. In some states, lawmakers have decriminalized marijuana in cases that involve possession of quantities that amount to no more than what could be consumed for personal use. In other words, laws in some states now recognize the difference between the pot user and the pot seller.

By decriminalizing marijuana, these states have not legalized the drug. Indeed, it is still illegal to possess marijuana in all fifty states. However, some states have made the penalties for possession so minor that the offender faces no real penalties at all except forfeiture of his or her pot.

A vocal segment of marijuana users believe decriminalization does not go far enough. They acknowledge that there may be health consequences associated with marijuana use, but they question whether that is reason enough to ban the substance. After all, legalization proponents point out, tobacco and alcohol also lead to addiction and harmful effects on health, and yet both those products are legal everywhere.

A protest sign decries the U.S. war on marijuana. Though still illegal in all states, marijuana possession has been decriminalized in some states.

R. Keith Stroup, the former executive director of NORML, says:

It is time we adopted a marijuana policy that reflects a distinction between use and abuse, and reflects the importance most Americans place on the right of the individual to be free from the overreaching power of government. Most would agree that the government has no business knowing what books we read, the subject of our telephone conversations, or how we conduct ourselves in the bedroom. Similarly, whether one smokes marijuana or drinks alcohol to relax is simply not an appropriate area of concern for the government.[45]

Ensuring the Purity

Public opinion polls show that a significant segment of the public is in agreement with Stroup. In 2003, a survey conducted by the Zogby International polling firm found that 40 percent of Americans believe "the government should treat marijuana more or less the same way it treats alcohol. It should regulate it, control it, tax it, and only make it illegal for children."[46]

Regulating the distribution of marijuana has been recommended by some political leaders, who suggest that government control over marijuana is one way to keep the gangs and drug lords out of the business. They point out that once alcohol was made illegal, the beer and liquor business was taken over by gangsters. When Prohibition was repealed, the gangsters were driven out of the business, and legal brewers and distillers took over.

Government regulation could also help ensure the purity of marijuana. Pot that is imported from other countries may be carrying bacteria that could spread disease. If pot becomes legal, federal agencies such as the Food and Drug Administration and the Department of Agriculture would be

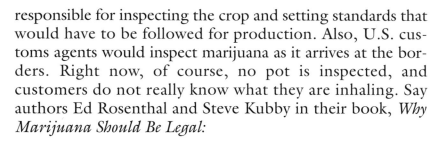

responsible for inspecting the crop and setting standards that would have to be followed for production. Also, U.S. customs agents would inspect marijuana as it arrives at the borders. Right now, of course, no pot is inspected, and customers do not really know what they are inhaling. Say authors Ed Rosenthal and Steve Kubby in their book, *Why Marijuana Should Be Legal*:

> The way Mexican marijuana is handled before it is shipped here creates opportunities for spoilage and disease. The marijuana is harvested and then dried in the open. Coca-Cola or another binding agent is poured over the dried pot, and the mass is pressed into bricks. Weeks may pass before these bricks of marijuana are brought over the border, allowing plenty of time for mold and bacteria to grow. In fact, the Centers for Disease Control has reported several epidemic-proportion outbreaks of illness resulting from contaminated or improperly handled marijuana. In one case in 1981, the marijuana was contaminated with animal feces and bacteria. As a result, eighty-five people were hospitalized for salmonella in Georgia, Alabama, California, Arizona, Massachusetts, Ohio, and Michigan. In another case, smokers developed lung problems after smoking improperly handled marijuana; the material had become moldy during shipment.[47]

When Prohibition was repealed in 1933, Congress quickly enacted a tax on alcohol that President Franklin Roosevelt used to finance the antipoverty programs of his New Deal that helped rescue Americans from the Great Depression. Since then, consumers of beer, wine, and liquor have continued to pay heavy taxes on the beverages. Proponents of legalizing marijuana suggest that if the government regulates the marijuana business, billions of dollars in new tax revenue could be raised. Most Americans would benefit, because the other taxes they pay would be reduced. "Control it, regulate

The National Organization for the Reform of Marijuana Laws, or NORML, was founded in 1970 by R. Keith Stroup, a young lawyer who had worked for the U.S. Commission on Product Safety, which was established to protect consumers from dangerous or faulty products. Stroup started using marijuana as a college student. While working as a consumer advocate, he conceived of the idea of an organization to speak up for the rights of marijuana consumers.

As of 2005, NORML founder R. Keith Stroup (right) no longer heads the group.

The organization initially met with some success. In 1972, the National Commission on Marijuana, which had been appointed by President Richard Nixon, recommended that people who possess less than an ounce (28.3g) of the drug should not be prosecuted. NORML brought the report to the attention of state legislatures, and due to NORML's efforts, five states—Alaska, California, Colorado, Maine, and Ohio—removed criminal penalties for possession of small amounts. In recent years, though, most political leaders have been hesitant to decriminalize marijuana, and NORML's role has changed. Now, the organization serves mostly as an unofficial legal advisor to its twelve thousand members, giving them tips on what to do if they are arrested or forced to submit to drug tests.

Stroup stepped down in 2005. He was replaced as NORML director by Allen St. Pierre, who had served as Stroup's deputy for the previous decade.

it, tax it," said former New Mexico governor Gary Johnson, who has called for the legalization of marijuana as well as other drugs. Johnson has also suggested that if marijuana is made legal, many drinkers would turn instead to pot. Johnson said he regards marijuana as a far safer substance than alcohol and tobacco. "Marijuana is never going to have the devastating effects on us that alcohol and tobacco have on us," he said. "If marijuana is legalized, alcohol abuse goes down, because people will have a substance choice."[48]

The Frankfurt Resolution

In many other countries, people are given a substance choice. The trend started in Europe in 1990, when drug abuse experts from four European cities—Amsterdam in the Netherlands, Frankfurt and Hamburg in Germany, and Zurich in Switzerland—met in Frankfurt to discuss ways of combating addiction. They concluded that the zeal to arrest, prosecute, and imprison drug offenders had not worked. The group of drug experts, who would form the organization European Cities on Drug Policy, found that most drug users are not criminals, and throwing them in jail exposes them to real criminals, making it more likely they would break laws when they are released from prison. The representatives at the Frankfurt conference suggested that it may be wiser to let people use drugs legally but to conduct public campaigns advising them of the risks and offering them programs to beat their addictions—much the same way alcohol and tobacco use is treated worldwide. They issued the Frankfurt Resolution, which says:

> Drug using is for the majority of users a temporary part of their biography, which can be overcome within the process of maturing out of addiction. Drug policy may not render this process more difficult, but it must support this process. . . . A drug policy fighting against addiction exclusively with the criminal law and the compulsion to abstinence and offering abstinence only has failed. . . . Criminalization is a counterpart to drug

Patrons at a Dutch coffee house take hits of pot from a bong. Pot can legally be sold and used in the Netherlands, but only in such cafes, not on the street.

aid and drug therapy and is a burden for police and justice they cannot carry. . . . The aid for drug users must no longer be threatened by criminal law. . . . It is necessary to lay stress on harm reduction and repressive forms of intervention must be reduced to the absolute necessary minimum.[49]

Lawmakers in many European countries have adopted the spirit of the Frankfurt Resolution, particularly when it applies to marijuana use. The nations of Germany, Belgium, Denmark, Greece, Ireland, Holland, Portugal, Spain, and England have declared that use of marijuana is not a criminal offense. Marijuana use in Italy remains a crime, but no penalty is assessed on the defendant. However, trafficking in drugs in those countries as well as others remains a crime; France, Greece, and Italy retain the stiffest laws, with sentences of up to twenty years for major traffickers.

As for the individual pot smoker, though, personal use in those European countries is treated as simply something that some people do. The Netherlands is regarded as having the most liberal pot laws in Europe. In the city of Amsterdam, use of marijuana and hashish in public coffee houses is permitted, although it cannot be used on the streets. Author Brian Preston describes his experience in Amsterdam while researching his book, *Pot Planet: Adventures in Global Marijuana Culture:*

> Buying and smoking good pot in the coffee shops of Amsterdam, you can get high in comfort, stumble into the street, and ask a cop for directions. I said, "Excuse

Many European nations have decriminalized marijuana use. This Dutch street sign warns that smoking pot on the street will incur a fine of fifty euros (about sixty-three dollars).

EVERTSENSTRAA
stadsdeel de baarsje

blowverbod
wegens overlast in de buurt

me" to get the attention of a cop one time, and he smiled back and said, "You are excused." I knew at that moment I reeked of weed, and I knew what an American activist had meant when he told me that sometimes in Amsterdam he felt like hugging the police.[50]

But has it worked? Have the European countries that abide by the spirit of the Frankfurt Resolution seen their addiction rates decline, or has much of Europe simply turned into a safe harbor for stoners? There is dispute over the success of the Frankfurt Resolution. DEA administrator Karen P. Tandy insists that drug use in Europe is spiraling upward. In the Netherlands, for example, Tandy says marijuana use has tripled among eighteen- to twenty-year-olds in the years since pot has been decriminalized. And she says Dutch officials are rethinking their marijuana policy. She points out that outside Amsterdam, many towns have passed local laws prohibiting use of marijuana in coffee houses. Without legal pot to entice customers, she says, coffee houses have been going out of business all over the Netherlands. "Almost all Dutch towns have a cannabis policy, and 73 percent of them have a no-tolerance policy toward the coffee houses,"[51] she says.

But other officials suggest that the policy of the Netherlands (sometimes called Holland) has worked. Gary Johnson, the former New Mexico governor, says:

> Holland is the only country in the world that has a rational drug policy. I had always heard that Holland, where marijuana is decriminalized and controlled, had out-of-control drug use, abuse and crime. But when I researched it, I learned that's untrue. It's propaganda. Holland has 60 percent of the drug use—both hard drugs and marijuana—the United States has. They have a quarter of the crime rate, a quarter the homicide rate, a quarter the violent crime rate, and a tenth the incarceration rate.[52]

The 420 Rallies

Each April 20, thousands of American college students stage demonstrations on their campuses to rally for the type of marijuana laws that have been adopted in the Netherlands and other European countries. The tradition has its roots in San Rafael, California, where starting in 1971 a group of high school students met each day at 4:20 P.M. to smoke marijuana. That led other students to stage so-called 420 events. Eventually, the tradition was adopted on college campuses, and April 20—4-20 on the calendar—was set aside as an unofficial holiday to pay tribute to marijuana and rally for liberalization of marijuana laws.

For the most part, college officials frown on the events because, along with the demonstrating and speechmaking, there is always a copious amount of marijuana smoked by the members of the audience. In 2005, one thousand students gathered for a 420 event on the campus of the University of Colorado in Boulder, despite rainy conditions. "If it wasn't raining, this place would be even more packed,"[53] said Mason Tvert, director of the marijuana advocacy group Safer Alternatives for Enjoyable Recreation.

Across town, speakers at another 420 rally urged the repeal of a city ordinance that requires people arrested for marijuana possession to pay a fine of five dollars. That is a very minor penalty, and actually, Colorado is one of a handful of states that have decriminalized marijuana possession to some degree. In Colorado, first-time offenders arrested for possession of a small amount of pot do not face jail time. Other states that have eliminated jail time for first-time offenders charged with possession of small quantities are Alaska, California, Maine, Minnesota, Mississippi, Nebraska, Nevada, New York, Ohio, Oregon, and West Virginia. Many other states maintain laws that include jail sentences, although in practice most judges will not send first-time offenders to prison if they are convicted of possessing small quantities. Instead, those offenders are most

Legalizing Hemp

The Marijuana Tax Act of 1937 helped drive hemp farmers out of business by assessing high fees on the production of cannabis. What is more, the Controlled Substances Act of 1970 said that marijuana has no legal purpose. However, in recent years proponents of hemp farming have started looking forward to the day when they can once again raise cannabis as a crop.

In 2003, the DEA issued an interpretation of the Controlled Substances Act that said hemp could be cultivated as long as the plants contain just microscopic traces of THC, the chemical that provides the high to marijuana users. To raise cannabis, hemp growers would have to obtain a permit from the agency, but by 2006 the DEA had not yet issued any permits.

Meanwhile, at least twenty-five countries do permit hemp farming. In Canada, for example, some 12,250 acres (4,957ha) produced hemp in 2000, according to the Hemp Industries Association. The Romanians are believed to grow the most hemp in the world with some 40,000 acres (16,188ha) devoted to the crop.

Many countries allow hemp farming, and hemp seeds now appear in many food products like these.

Pot and the Presidents

In 1992, as Bill Clinton campaigned for the presidency, reports surfaced that he had experimented with marijuana while attending Oxford University in England. Clinton was forced to admit his marijuana use, although he acknowledged only a brief episode with the drug and even claimed not to have inhaled the smoke. The public was dubious of that story but did not hold it against him. He was elected president in 1992 and reelected four years later.

In 2000, as he campaigned for the presidency, George W. Bush acknowledged his own substance abuse problems, although he admitted publicly only to a prior drinking problem. And yet, in 2005, author Doug Wead reported in his book, *The Raising of a President*, that Bush had smoked marijuana but refused to answer questions from reporters about his use of the substance. "I wouldn't answer the marijuana questions," Bush told Wead. "You know why? Because I don't want some little kid doing what I tried."

BBC News, "Bush Hinted at Use of Marijuana," February 21, 2005. http://news.bbc.co.uk/2/hi/americas/4282799.stm.

likely to receive brief sentences of probation. In fact, many states also maintain programs that will expunge the offenders' criminal records if they stay out of trouble. Still, in most states the laws carry the possibility of jail time, and the judges do have the discretion of locking up first-time offenders.

Meanwhile, it is likely that in many states, second-time offenders will see the insides of their local jailhouses—even if their second offense, like their first, includes the possession of no more than a single marijuana cigarette. Indeed, legislatures in twenty-eight states have enacted laws providing jail terms of up to a year for repeat offenders. And if the amount of marijuana in possession is more than a few joints—typically an ounce (28.3g) or more—the penalties escalate further. For example, in Georgia, possession of an ounce of marijuana is punishable by as much as ten years in prison.

Federal penalties can be strict. The 1970 Controlled Substances Act eliminated mandatory minimum penalties for marijuana possession, but in 1986 Congress passed the Anti–Drug Abuse Act, establishing mandatory minimum sentences in most drug cases prosecuted in federal courts. The law was aimed at putting major drug traffickers behind bars, but all drugs, including marijuana, were included in the legislation. In addition, all manner of offenses, including possession of a small amount of pot, were covered by the law.

The Anti–Drug Abuse Act

Typically, the DEA, the Federal Bureau of Investigation, and other federal law enforcement agencies do not target individual users of pot. Rather, federal agencies go after big-time drug lords. Still, penalties for simple possession are on the books, and individuals can be prosecuted in federal courts. Under federal law, a first-time offender arrested in possession of a single marijuana cigarette faces up to a year in prison, although most judges will not levy that harsh a sentence. However, the second-time offender arrested in possession of a small amount of pot faces a mandatory minimum of fifteen days in jail, and a third-time offender must spend at least ninety days and as long as three years locked up in a federal penitentiary.

The 1986 law was passed following the death of Len Bias, a college basketball star who celebrated his selection in the National Basketball Association draft by going to a party and ingesting a fatal dose of cocaine. The nation was shocked by the death of Bias. Responding to intense public pressure, federal lawmakers felt compelled to come down hard on all drug

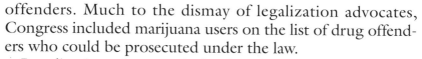

offenders. Much to the dismay of legalization advocates, Congress included marijuana users on the list of drug offenders who could be prosecuted under the law.

Legalization advocates insist that the 1986 federal law, as well as the many state statutes that include jail sentences for offenders, has resulted in a tremendous number of people serving prison terms—both short and long—for marijuana offenses. Indeed, according to the U.S. Department of Justice, about seven hundred thousand people a year are arrested on marijuana offenses, and about sixty thousand of them are sentenced to spend time in prison. NORML executive director Allen St. Pierre insists that many of those individuals serving time are guilty of nothing more than possessing small amounts of marijuana that they had intended for their own use. He says:

> America's policy-makers need to immediately stop arresting and incarcerating such a huge portion of the citizenry, most notably for possessing and cultivating small amounts of marijuana. Rather than waste valuable public resources on introducing otherwise law-abiding citizens into the criminal justice system, the government should establish legal controls which tax and regulate responsible adult marijuana use.[54]

Debate Will Continue

The debate over the legalization or decriminalization of marijuana is not likely to be settled soon. While both sides appear to make valid arguments, few legislators are prone to risk their political futures by appearing to favor legalization of a dangerous drug. Meanwhile, it is certain that the medical marijuana debate will continue as well. Even though the U.S. Supreme Court has ruled on the matter, advocates of medical marijuana have vowed to continue the fight, and they also plan to continue using marijuana to ease their suffering. Regardless of how marijuana is viewed, it cannot be denied that very serious health issues are associated with pot, and until scientific evidence surfaces that definitively proves marijuana is not as harmful as it is believed to be, lawmakers would have no reason to budge off their steadfast position that marijuana is an illegal substance and should remain that way.

Notes

Introduction: Marijuana: The Drug That Never Goes Away

1. John P. Walters, "No Surrender: The Drug War Saves Lives," *National Review*, September 14, 2004, p. 41.
2. Quoted in Hal Marcovitz, "Two Men Get 5 Years in Drug Ring; over 3,000 Pounds of Marijuana Brought to Bucks Since 2001," *Allentown (PA) Morning Call*, March 17, 2006, p. B-1.

Chapter 1: Marijuana Through the Ages

3. Quoted in Edward M. Brecher, *Licit and Illicit Drugs*. Mount Vernon, NY: Consumers Union, 1972, p. 298.
4. Quoted in Brecher, *Licit and Illicit Drugs*, p. 408.
5. Quoted in Larry Sloman, *Reefer Madness: A History of Marijuana*. New York: St. Martin's Griffin, 1998, p. 48.
6. Quoted in Brecher, *Licit and Illicit Drugs*, p. 411.
7. Dan Wakefield, *New York in the Fifties*. Boston: Houghton Mifflin, 1992, p. 177.
8. Wakefield, *New York in the Fifties*, p. 177.
9. Andrew Peyton Thomas, "Mea Culpas on Marijuana," the *American Enterprise Online*, May/June 1997. www.taemag.com/issues/articleid.16187/article_detail.asp.
10. Quoted in the *New York Times*, "Bethel Pilgrims Smoke 'Grass' and Some Take LSD to 'Groove,'" August 18, 1969, p. 25.
11. Quoted in the *New York Times*, "Bethel Pilgrims Smoke 'Grass' and Some Take LSD to 'Groove,'" p. 25.
12. Kristy Graver, "Tela Ropa Lives! Writer Who Spent Her Teen Years at Local Head Shop Laments Its Passing," *Pittsburgh Post-Gazette*, May 19, 2004, p. C-2.

Chapter 2: How Marijuana Affects the Brain, Body, and Behavior

13. Quoted in Vanessa Grigoriadis, "The Most Stoned Kids on the Most Stoned Day on the Most Stoned Campus on Earth," *Rolling Stone*, September 16, 2004, p. 70.

14. Joseph M. Rey, Andres Martin, and Peter Krabman, "Is the Party Over? Cannabis and Juvenile Psychiatric Disorder: The Past 10 Years," *Journal of the American Academy of Child and Adolescent Psychiatry*, October 2004, p. 1,194.

15. Rey, Martin, and Krabman, "Is the Party Over?" p. 20.

16. National Highway Traffic Safety Administration, "Drugs and Human Performance Fact Sheets: Cannabis/Marijuana." www.nhtsa.dot.gov/people/injury/research/job 185drugs/cannabis.htm.

17. National Highway Traffic Safety Administration, "Drugs and Human Performance Fact Sheets."

18. Quoted in Theresa D. McClellan, "Teen Gets Jail Time for Fatal Crash," *Grand Rapids (MI) Press*, March 22, 2006. www.mlive.com/news/grpress/index.ssf?/base/news-28/ 11430424515160.xml&coll=6.

19. Quoted in Associated Press, "Report: Pilot in Fresno Plane Crash Had Marijuana in His System," *San Jose (CA) Mercury News*, March 26, 2006. www.mercurynews.com/mld/ mercurynews/news/breaking_news/14188506.htm.

20. Quoted in NPR Online, "Transcript of NPR's Interview with Armstrong Biographer Laurence Bergreen," 1997. www.npr.org/programs/specials/hotter/interview.html.

21. Peter A. Fried, "Behavioral Outcomes in Preschool and School-Age Children Exposed to Marijuana: A Review and Speculative Interpretation," National Institutes of Health, p. 242. www.nida.nih.gov/pdf/monographs/monograph 164/242-260_Fried.pdf.

22. Rey, Martin, and Krabman, "Is the Party Over?" *Journal of the American Academy of Child and Adolescent Psychiatry*, p. 1,194.

Chapter 3: The Culture of Pot

23. Quoted in *Billings (MT) Gazette*, "Pilot Spots Big Swath of Marijuana Growing Near Sheriff's Facility," August 21, 2005. www.billingsgazette/com/newdex.php?display=red-news/ 2005/08/21/build/nation/98-pot-sheriff.inc.

24. U.S. Substance Abuse and Mental Health Services Administration, *2003 National Survey on Drug Use and Health*. http://oas.samhsa.gov/nhsda.htm#NHSDAinfo.

25. National Drug Intelligence Center, *National Drug Threat Assessment 2005: Marijuana*. www.usdoj.gov/ndic/pubs11 /12620/marijuana.htm.

26. Quoted in Randal C. Archibold, "Officials Find Drug Tunnel with Surprising Amenities," *New York Times*, January 27, 2006, p. A-14.

27. Karen Tandy, "The Government's Marijuana Suppression Program Reduces Drug Use," testimony before the U.S. House Appropriations Committee, Washington, DC, March 24, 2004.

28. Pennsylvania Crime Commission, *Organized Crime in Pennsylvania: A Decade of Change*, 1990, p. 201.

29. Quoted in BBC News, "Sir Paul Reveals Beatles Drug Use," June 4, 2004. http://news.bbc.co.uk/1/hi/entertainment /music/3769511.stm.

30. Quoted in BBC News, "Sir Paul Reveals Beatles Drug Use."

31. Grigoriadis, "The Most Stoned Kids on the Most Stoned Day on the Most Stoned Campus on Earth," p. 70.

32. Quoted in Sloman, *Reefer Madness*, p. 262.

33. Quoted in Sloman, *Reefer Madness*, p. 263.

Chapter 4: Medical Marijuana

34. Quoted in Susan Campbell, "Living with HIV—and Maybe Only Because of Cannabis," *Hartford (CT) Courant*, May 18, 2001, p. D-2.

35. Quoted in Stephen Henderson, "Court Loss for Medical Marijuana," *Philadelphia Inquirer*, June 7, 2005, p. A-1.

36. Quoted in Brian Preston, *Pot Planet: Adventures in Global Marijuana Culture*. New York: Grove, 2002, p. 257.

37. Quoted in Preston, *Pot Planet*, p. 255.

38. Quoted in Preston, *Pot Planet*, p. 255.

39. Quoted in *Consumer Reports*, "Marijuana as Medicine," The Science of Medical Marijuana, May 1997. www.medmjscience.org/Pages/history/consumerreports.html.

40. Quoted in *Consumer Reports*, "Marijuana as Medicine."

41. Quoted in John Cloud, "Is Pot Good for You?" *Time*, November 4, 2002, p. 62.

42. Quoted in *Consumer Reports*, "Marijuana as Medicine."

43. Quoted in Henderson, "Court Loss for Medical Marijuana," p. A-1.

44. Quoted in Erica Werner, "Medical Marijuana Advocates Implore Congress for Reform," Associated Press, *San Jose (CA) Mercury News*, May 4, 2005. www.mercurynews.com/mld/mercurynews/news/local/states/california/northern_california/11564531.htm.

Chapter 5: The Debate over Legalization

45. R. Keith Stroup, testimony before the U.S. House Subcommittee on Criminal Justice, Drug Policy and Human Resources, Committee on Government Reform, July 13, 1999.

46. Ethan A. Nadelman, "An End to Marijuana Prohibition: The Drive to Legalize Picks Up," *National Review*, July 12, 2004, pp. 29–30.

47. Ed Rosenthal and Steve Kubby, *Why Marijuana Should Be Legal*. New York: Thunder's Mouth, 2003, p. 62.

48. Quoted in "New Mexico Governor Calls for Legalizing Drugs," CNN, October 6, 1999. www.cnn.com/US/99 10/06/legalizing.drugs.01.

49. Quoted in National Organization for the Reform of Marijuana Laws, "European Drug Policy," 2002. www.norml. org/index.cfm?Group_ID=4415#europe.

50. Preston, *Pot Planet*, p. 160.

51. Karen P. Tandy, "Marijuana: The Myths Are Killing Us," U.S. Drug Enforcement Administration. www.usdoj.gov/dea/pubs/pressrel/pr042605.html.
52. Quoted in Preston, *Pot Planet*, p. 146.
53. Quoted in Brad Turner, "Pot Activists Gather for Annual 420 Event," *Longmont (CO) Daily Times-Call*, April 21, 2005. www.longmontfyi.com/Local-Story.asp?id=1382.
54. Quoted in National Organization for the Reform of Marijuana Laws, "America's Prison Population Hits All-Time High," November 12, 2004. www.norml.org/index.cfm?Group_ID=6334.

ORGANIZATIONS TO CONTACT

Drug Enforcement Administration (DEA)
2401 Jefferson Davis Hwy. Alexandria, VA 22301
(202) 307-1000
www.usdoj.gov/dea

The U.S. Justice Department's chief antidrug law enforcement agency is charged with investigating the illegal narcotics trade in the United States and helping local police agencies with their antidrug efforts. The DEA's Web site includes many reports on efforts by the agency to break up marijuana rings.

European Monitoring Centre for Drugs and Drug Addiction
Rua da Cruz de Santa Apolónia 23-25 PT-1149-045 Lisbon, Portugal
(+351) 21 811 3000
http://eldd.emcdda.eu.int

Based in Portugal, the organization monitors narcotics use in Europe. Visitors to the Web site can download the report *Decriminalization in Europe? Recent Developments in Legal Approaches to Drug Use*, which provides a breakdown of how each country in Europe tolerates marijuana use.

Hemp Industries Association
PO Box 1080 Occidental, CA 95465
(707) 874-3648
www.thehia.org

The association supports efforts to legalize hemp farming in America. Visitors to the association's Web site can find a history of hemp farming and updates on the laws regulating the cultivation of cannabis for use in textiles, rope, and other products.

National Drug Intelligence Center
319 Washington St., 5th Fl. Johnstown, PA 15901-1622
(814) 532-4601
www.usdoj.gov/ndic

A part of the Justice Department, the agency provides intelligence on drug trends to government leaders and law enforcement agencies. Each year, the agency produces the *National Drug Threat Assessment*, which includes information on marijuana use in America.

National Institute on Drug Abuse (NIDA)
6001 Executive Blvd., Rm. 5213 Bethesda, MD 20892-9561
(301) 443-1124
www.nida.nih.gov

Part of the National Institutes of Health, the NIDA's mission is to help finance scientific research projects that study addiction trends and treatment of chronic drug users. The NIDA's report, *Marijuana Abuse*, can be downloaded from its Web site.

National Organization for the Reform of Marijuana Laws (NORML)
1600 K St. NW, Suite 501 Washington, DC 20006-2832
(202) 483-550
www.norml.org

NORML's Web site contains news, position papers, statistics, and reports on marijuana use in America. Students can find a state-by-state breakdown of marijuana laws and the legal penalties faced by offenders.

White House Office of National Drug Control Policy/Drug Policy Information Clearinghouse
PO Box 6000 Rockville, MD 20849-6000
(800) 666-3332
www.whitehousedrugpolicy.gov

The White House Office of National Drug Control Policy was established to develop a national strategy to combat illegal drug

use. The office is a liaison serving the different federal drug investigation and research agencies and helps provide information to
state and local agencies that fight drug abuse. The office has issued the report *What Americans Need to Know About
Marijuana*, which can be downloaded from its Web site.

FOR FURTHER READING

Books

Jamuna Carroll, ed., *Opposing Viewpoints: Marijuana*. Farmington Hills, MI: Greenhaven, 2006. Essays and articles on legalization issues, medical marijuana, and the health effects of the drug are included in this volume.

Rudolph J. Gerber, *Legalizing Marijuana: Drug Policy Reform and Prohibition Politics*. Westport, CT: Praeger, 2004. The author, a retired Arizona judge, argues that the war on drugs, particularly marijuana, has been an expensive failure. Gerber calls for legalization of medical marijuana as the first step toward a gradual decriminalization of the drug that would permit possession of small amounts for personal use.

Louise Gerdes, ed., *Marijuana*. San Diego: Greenhaven, 2002. Essays and articles covering many topics related to marijuana are included in the book, such as hemp production, decriminalization, addiction, health consequences, and whether pot is a gateway drug. The book also includes stories from pot users.

George McMahon and Christopher Largen, *Prescription Pot: A Leading Advocate's Heroic Battle to Legalize Medical Marijuana*. Far Hills, NJ: New Horizon, 2003. McMahon, who suffers from a rare bone disease, explains why he uses marijuana for medicinal purposes and examines the plight of others who seek pain relief through cannabis.

Terrence E. Poppa, *Drug Lord: A True Story*. Seattle: Demand, 1998. The book examines the story of Pablo Acosta, the Mexican drug lord who smuggled tons of marijuana across the border before he was killed in a shootout with police in 1987.

Brian Preston, *Pot Planet: Adventures in Global Marijuana Culture*. New York: Grove, 2002. Preston visited Holland, Morocco, England, Australia, Canada, and other countries to find out how different societies view marijuana use.

Ed Rosenthal and Steve Kubby, *Why Marijuana Should Be Legal.* New York: Thunder's Mouth, 2003. Rosenthal, a medical marijuana grower whose conviction touched off a storm of protests, provides his argument for why marijuana use should not be a crime.

Ed Rosenthal, ed., *Hemp Today.* Oakland, CA: Quick American Archives, 1994. The medical marijuana advocate turns his attention to hemp. The book—which is printed on paper milled from cannabis fibers—covers the history of cannabis farming in America and argues that hemp production is a legitimate industry that should be legalized.

Elizabeth Schleichert, *Marijuana.* Springfield, NJ: Enslow, 1996. The book includes a history of the drug as well as an overview of the effects of marijuana on human health. The author suggests peer pressure is responsible for marijuana use among teenagers and examines the cases of movie star Drew Barrymore and tennis player Jennifer Capriati, both of whom turned to marijuana to escape the pressures of being celebrities.

Larry Sloman, *Reefer Madness: A History of Marijuana.* New York: St. Martin's Griffin, 1998. The author provides a thorough history of marijuana use in America and interviews a number of people who are part of the pot culture.

Stephen P. Thompson, ed., *The War on Drugs: Opposing Viewpoints.* San Diego: Greenhaven, 1998. Efforts by the government, the police, and social services agencies to stamp out the use of marijuana and other drugs are examined in a number of essays and articles included in this volume; the issue of medical marijuana is the subject of six essays.

Periodicals

John Cloud, "Is Pot Good for You?" *Time*, November 4, 2002. The *Time* magazine cover story provides an in-depth examination of medical marijuana.

Vanessa Grigoriadis, "The Most Stoned Kids on the Most Stoned Day on the Most Stoned Campus on Earth," *Rolling Stone*,

September 16, 2004. The magazine interviewed pot-smoking students in the days leading up to the annual 420 celebration on the campus of the University of California–Santa Cruz.

Web Sites

Frontline, **PBS** (www.pbs.org/wgbh/pages/frontline/shows /dope). This companion Web site to the *Frontline* documentary "Busted: America's War on Marijuana" includes a history of marijuana use in America, the status of laws and sentencing trends, and interviews with marijuana growers serving prison terms.

Office of National Drug Control Policy (www.whitehouse-drugpolicy.gov/publications/drugfact/pulsechk/january04). The White House Office of National Drug Control Policy report *Pulse Check: National Trends in Drug Abuse* can be downloaded at this Web site. The report contains a city-by-city study of marijuana use in America, including the availability of the drug and its street price.

Index

PICTURE CREDITS

About the Author

Hal Marcovitz is a journalist who lives in Chalfont, Pennsylvania, with his wife, Gail, and daughters, Michelle and Ashley. He has written more than seventy books for young readers as well as the satirical novel *Painting the White House*.